Creating Capital Markets in Eastern Europe

Creating Capital Markets in Eastern Europe

edited by John R. Lampe

WW *Published by The Woodrow Wilson Center Press*

Distributed by The Johns Hopkins University Press

Woodrow Wilson Center Special Studies

The Woodrow Wilson Center Press
Editorial Offices
370 L'Enfant Promenade, S.W.
Suite 704
Washington, D.C. 20024-2518 U.S.A.
telephone 202-287-3000, ext. 218

Distributed by
The Johns Hopkins University Press
701 West 40th Street, Suite 275
Baltimore, Maryland 21211
order department telephone 1-800-537-5487

Library of Congress Cataloging-in-Publication Data

Creating capital markets in Eastern Europe / edited by John R. Lampe.
    p.   cm. — (Woodrow Wilson Center special studies)
    Includes index.
    ISBN 0-943875-42-0 (pbk. : alk. paper) : $10.95
    1. Capital market—Europe, Eastern—Congresses. 2. Europe,
Eastern—Economic policy—1989—Congresses. I. Lampe, John R.
II. Series.
HG5430.7.A3C74 1992
332.63'2'0947—dc20   92-26523
                                         CIP

The Woodrow Wilson International Center for Scholars

The Center is the "living memorial" of the United States of America to the nation's twenty-eighth president, Woodrow Wilson. The U.S. Congress established the Woodrow Wilson Center in 1968 as an international institute for advanced study, "symbolizing and strengthening the fruitful relationship between the world of learning and the world of public affairs." The Center opened in 1970 under its own presidentially appointed board of directors.

Woodrow Wilson Center Special Studies

The work of the Center's Fellows, Guest Scholars, and staff and presentations and discussions at the Center's conferences, seminars, and colloquia often deserve timely circulation as contributions to public understanding of issues of national and international importance. The Woodrow Wilson Center Special Studies series is intended to make such materials available to interested scholars, practitioners, and other readers. In all its activities, the Woodrow Wilson Center is a nonprofit, nonpartisan organization, supported financially by annual appropriations from the U.S. Congress, and by the contributions of foundations, corporations, and individuals. Conclusions or opinions expressed in Center publications and programs are those of the authors and speakers and do not necessarily reflect the views of the Center's staff, Fellows, Trustees, advisory groups, or any individuals or organizations that provide financial support to the Center.

v

Contents

Tables

Acknowledgments

This book had its origins in a conference "Creating Capital Markets in Eastern Europe," held September 20–22, 1991, in Sofia, Bulgaria. The conference was organized by the East European Studies program of the Woodrow Wilson International Center for Scholars, Washington, D.C., with the local assistance of the Center for the Study of Democracy, Sofia. Funds supporting the conference came from the Rockefeller Brothers Fund, from grants by the U.S. Congress to the Woodrow Wilson Center, and from the Bulgarian branch of the Soros Foundation's Open Society Fund.

Support for publishing this book came from funds awarded to the Woodrow Wilson Center's East European Studies program by Congress under the terms of the Soviet and East European Research and Training Act of 1983.

The editor gratefully acknowledges the assistance of the staff members of the East European Studies program in the preparation of this book: Kristin Hunter, program assistant; Steven Langmuir, program intern; and Maya Latynski, program associate.

Introduction

John R. Lampe

The abrupt collapse of communist regimes throughout Eastern Europe during the last months of 1989 created widespread hopes for a comparably rapid transition to political democracy and market economies. New parties appeared almost overnight, essentially free elections were held everywhere except Romania, and new entrepreneurs opened shops and other small businesses. Overtures to the European Community from Poland and Hungary hardly seemed premature. Three years later, it is clear that there is more to political democracy than holding multiparty elections and more to a market economy than authorizing private enterprise and property rights.

The promise of privatization and free competition (they are still the only alternatives in the long run) remains compelling, but its fulfillment seems elusive in the short run. Financial institutions and instruments increasingly appear to be the key to the privatization of large enterprises, for without access to adequate credit, investment capital, and convertible currency, no entrepreneur has a chance to start a sizeable firm or, as is more likely to be the case, to change the course of an erstwhile state enterprise.

The obvious mechanism for mobilizing capital seemed at first to be a Western-style stock market. "Creating Capital Markets in Eastern Europe," the Woodrow Wilson Center conference in September 1991, certainly started from that premise. Staged in Sofia, Bulgaria, at the originally Japanese-owned Hotel Vitosha, now appropriately a Bulgarian enterprise, the conference brought together bankers, stock market analysts, economists, and businesspeople from the United States and Europe.

The representative selection of conference papers in this volume draws on each of the four sessions of the conference. Their topics were:

1. The pre-1945 financial history of Eastern Europe and the post-1945 financial history of the major Western capital markets;
2. The progress of privatization to date, particularly in mobilizing domestic or foreign capital throughout the region;
3. The role of present and future stock markets, including the various strategies for issuing shares; and
4. The structure of commercial and investment banking that would best allocate credit and capital.

The chapters that follow frequently suggest connections among these four areas. They also support the two general conclusions on which most participants seemed to agree: First, the slow pace of privatization must be accelerated if the transition to a market economy is to succeed during this decade. Second, a commercial banking system restructured along Continental lines offers a better prospect for such an acceleration than do dominant stock markets based on the Anglo-American model.

The capital markets that emerged in Eastern Europe before and after World War I relied more on banks than on stock exchanges. In her survey of the interwar period (Chapter 1), Alice Teichova notes that stock exchanges were soon established in Warsaw, Belgrade, Zagreb, and Ljubljana, as well as in Bratislava and Brno. They joined prewar counterparts in Budapest and Prague, but none was as large as the Vienna exchange. Only in Czechoslovakia did a body of strict legislation emerge to regulate operations. In none of these exchanges, Teichova adds, did the value of company shares traded exceed the value of other securities. Industry's major access to capital and credit came instead from the large investment banks, domestic and foreign. Foreign banks were the predominant investors in the shares that were issued—but rarely traded on local stock markets—for enterprises in mining and heavy industry.

Foreign loans were available to the interwar East European governments, but on stricter terms and at higher rates of interest than during either the pre-1914 period or the present era of standby agreements for International Monetary Fund credit. During the 1920s, central banks nonetheless followed the same restrictive practice of currency emissions at overvalued exchange rates as they had before 1914. No international institution comparable to the World Bank was in sight. East European governments were left to spend the bulk of their loans on debt service or noneconomic projects, as they had before World War I. Exports were again overpriced, and the mobilization of domestic capital, even by aggressive investment banks, was made more expensive.[1] The depression of the 1930s restricted currency exchange and reduced access to capital markets still further. By the end of that decade, Teichova rightly concludes, a free market economy existed nowhere in the region, not even in Czechoslovakia. This was the unpromising financial legacy, particularly for any reliance on stock markets, with which all the East European economies entered the post-World War II period. Private enterprises in restricted markets that rested on shaky financial foundations, even before the ravages of World War II, are unfortunately all that Eastern Europe can call on for an indigenous precommunist model.

The current health of the Western model is of course open to question. In his review of the four major Western stock markets (Chapter 2), Maurice E. May, of Gardner & Preston Moss, Inc., Boston, identifies significant problems facing the New York, London, Frankfurt, and Tokyo stock markets in the 1990s. The New York and London exchanges have given up the fixed commissions that once guaranteed large, predictable profits. New York must deal with the further pressure from American banks and brokerage houses to consolidate in the face of international competition. London's "International Stock Exchange" must come to terms with the monetary restraint likely to result from the Maastricht agreement. The volatile Tokyo exchange continues to risk pricing issues at a ratio of debt to equity higher than the Western norm. Both Tokyo and the much smaller Frankfurt exchange are criticized for being dominated by an inner circle of bankers.

Western banks and the Anglo-American brokerage firms have in any case proved reluctant to invest in East European equities. May points out that there are enduring institutional barriers to placements in unproven shares or markets, particularly "investment plans" that overstate the attractiveness of established markets and undervalue emerging markets such as those in Eastern Europe. Perhaps, he concludes, the so-called country funds, which offer shares in mutual funds designated for states such as Taiwan, Brazil, and Mexico, offer hope that more Western portfolio investment will be channeled into East European stocks and their exchanges.

Western capital continues to enter Eastern Europe more commonly as direct investment from banks or companies. Dirk W.

Damrau, of Salomon Brothers, Inc., New York, writes in Chapter 3 that such investment is "indispensable to the creation of advanced, industrialized free-market–oriented economies in Eastern Europe." He begins his survey of Eastern Europe's three northernmost countries, Hungary, Poland, and Czechoslovakia, however, by pointing out that the projected flow of direct investment to all three of these economies for 1991 is less than half of the individual totals for Malaysia, Portugal, and Turkey. He goes on to identify a series of interrelated obstacles to privatization and foreign investment. Major investors are reluctant to enter economies with no significant domestic constituency for their presence and cannot anticipate sufficient control of management in enterprises "in which workers, former managers, and the state retain majority stakes." Such is likely to be the case even after privatization under the voucher scheme that has been promised in Czechoslovakia and which is also a possibility in Poland. In Poland and Hungary, rapid privatization of large firms is not a prospect, with the political struggle over restitution to previous owners adding to the delay. Damrau also notes the enduring difficulties surrounding currency conversion and debt settlement, as well as the lack of a clear comparative advantage for the region. The costs of establishing any new enterprise, at least in the capital cities, have now risen to West European levels. Damrau concludes with some encouraging words for prospects in Hungary and Bulgaria. However, he laments that the opening of new stock exchanges has been given more attention than the establishment of a viable system of commercial banks.

Opened in June 1990, the first and most active East European exchange is in Budapest. In Chapter 4, József Rotyis offers an overview of the Budapest exchange's limited but growing operations. Only eighteen companies were trading shares by September 1991, and most of the customers were foreign. Daily trade volume nonetheless was 250 percent greater during the first six months of 1991 than it was in the last six months of 1990. Rotyis identifies a series of challenges for the future and lessons from existing experience. Two lessons—to start simply and slowly, and to avoid copying a single foreign system completely—were endorsed at the Woodrow Wilson Center conference by James Shapiro of the New York Stock Exchange. Shapiro recalled the "stock exchange fetish" of the initial post-1989 visitors from Eastern Europe and his cautionary responses. At the same time, Shapiro reminded conference attendees of the basic utility of a stock exchange in pricing assets, educating customers in the market mechanism, and in the short run taking assets away from the state. Unfortunately, Rotyis noted, the first fully privatized enterprise was not expected to appear on the Hungarian exchange until 1992. Stimulation from stock markets, several discussants observed, is more likely to be a consequence of a successful transition to a market economy than a cause of it in Hungary.

The more important partner for newly privatized or newly created East European enterprises would in any case appear to be a genuinely commercial banking system tied to an independent central bank capable of the monetary discipline necessary to maintain a convertible currency. In Chapter 5, Marvin R. Jackson's review of company management and capital markets across the entire region makes this case at some length. Like Rotyis and others, Jackson cautions against any attempt to copy one Western country's financial institutions *in toto*. He nonetheless finds the Continental system, personified by the German banks, as the best model from which to work. These are universal banks, combining commercial operations and investment as American banks were forbidden to do by the Glass-Steagall Act of 1934 until the present, when only a few exceptions are being approved. The German banks, rather than the small Frankfurt stock market described in May's chapter, accounted for some 90 percent of net investment capital raised outside German enterprises throughout the 1970s and 1980s. Within these German firms, upper limits on the holdings of any one shareholder discourage the takeovers so familiar in the United States and also increase bank leverage. Bank ownership of company shares and the right to vote depositor shares also help explain the prominence of bank officials on the supervisory boards of German companies.

Replacing bureaucrats with bankers seems a fine idea, but how can a set of universal banks in the East European economies be established without burdening those banks with the credit demands of surviving but unprofitable state enterprises? This is the dilemma addressed in the last and longest chapter in this volume. Alfredo Thorne of the World Bank takes the recent Bulgarian experience as a case study and, speaking for himself, prescribes a dual system of banks. One set of Bulgarian banks would be privatized quickly and then authorized to lend *exclusively* to private enterprises. Another set of banks still under state control would struggle with schemes to restructure unprofitable state enterprises, and absorb their past bad debts as losses to the state budget or the enterprise itself. This "dual track" would encourage successful private enterprises by affording them easy access to credit. It would also confine the damage and risk from the old losers while offering them a chance to survive. Besides these advantages, Thorne cites the promotion of savings in the private banks as a further gain. His scheme represents the sort of adjustment to the Western model that seems essential if this unprecedented transition from state socialism to market capitalism is to make significant progress during the balance of the decade.

Note

[1]John R. Lampe and Marvin R. Jackson, *Balkan Economic History, 1550–1950* (Bloomington: Indiana University Press, 1982), chapters 6 and 9.

Chapter 1

Interwar Capital Markets in Central and Southeastern Europe

Alice Teichova

A general lack of investment capital has been a fundamental problem for Central and Southeastern Europe throughout the nineteenth and twentieth centuries. As a result of World War I, the supply of both domestic and foreign capital declined at the same time that the demand for capital rose dramatically. In this chapter, the author discusses interwar capital markets in the context of that general situation, outlining the foundation and functions of stock exchanges, and then discussing the crucial role of banks in the capital and credit movements of the interwar period.

This contribution draws largely from two research projects supported by the Economic and Social Research Council (UK), for which I express my thanks. In the first project, on the economic history of Eastern Europe, I participated on a research team directed by Michael C. Kaser, the efforts of which resulted in the publication of M.C. Kaser et al., eds., *The Economic History of Eastern Europe, 1919–75*, 3 vols. (Oxford, England: Oxford University Press, 1985, 1986). The second research project, on multinational companies in interwar Eastern Europe, which I directed, resulted in the publication of A. Teichova and P.L. Cottrell, eds., *International Business and Central Europe, 1919–39* (Leicester, England: Leicester University Press, 1983). I am also grateful to Cambridge University Press for permission to draw from my book, *An Economic Background to Munich, International Business and Czechoslovakia, 1918–38* (1974), and from my contribution to P. Mathias and S. Pollard, eds., *The Cambridge Economic History of Europe* (1989), vol. 8, "East Central and Southeast Europe, 1919–39," pp. 887–983. In addition I drew on material from my book, *Kleinstaaten im Spannungsfeld der Großmächte: Wirtschaft und Politik in Mittel- und Südosteuropa in der Zwischenkriegszeit* (Munich: R. Oldenbourg Verlag, 1988).

Pre-1914 and Interwar Stock Exchanges

In pursuit of the Habsburg Empire's late–eighteenth-century policy of emulating and attempting to catch up with the advanced economies of Western Europe, the Empress Maria Theresa founded a stock exchange in Vienna by the decree (Patent) of August 1, 1771. Thus appeared the first stock exchange in Central Europe—three centuries after the establishment of the world's first stock exchange (in Antwerp), two centuries after the founding of the Royal Exchange in London, more than half a century after the start of the Paris stock exchange, but a quarter-century before the initiation of the Berlin stock exchange. Exactly one century later (1871), the Prague stock exchange opened its doors, although its establishment had been proposed at the same time as Vienna's. The Budapest exchange had been established in 1864.

After World War I, stock exchanges started to function in other towns of the new successor states in Central and Southeastern Europe (Belgrade, Bratislava, Brno, Ljubljana, Warsaw, and Zagreb). They competed for business, above all, with Vienna. Dealings in securities, bills of exchange, and foreign currencies outpaced the trade in stock shares on all these exchanges. Even in Vienna the number of shares traded on the stock exchange was at no time after 1900 greater than the number of other securities traded.

Postwar hyperinflation delayed normalization until 1926–27, by which time most currencies in Eastern Europe had been stabilized and central banks established in the capitals of the successor states. Although the finances of Austria, Hungary, Poland, and Bulgaria were under international supervision, and the new central banks were to be independent of the state, the banks and their governments, nevertheless, had to act as lenders of last resort, especially after the ill-fated "franc speculation" of 1924–25 that rocked the Viennese financial center to its foundations. The Vienna stock exchange never really recovered entirely from the franc speculation, yet numerous Czech, Hungarian, Yugoslav, and Polish securities continued to be traded there. In fact, the new exchanges in the successor states actively sought to cultivate and consolidate business ties with Vienna, which, despite all its setbacks, retained many links to international markets. The Vienna stock exchange itself took the initiative in 1927–28 to unify the conditions and regulations for membership in all these exchanges. The financial crisis of 1931, however, put an end to these efforts at cooperation among capital markets in Central and Southeastern Europe.

Grain exchanges similar to those existing in Vienna, Prague, Budapest, and Belgrade since the late nineteenth century were also established after 1918 in Bratislava, Brno, Olomouc, Bucharest, Timişoara, Novisad, and Zagreb. Given the relative backwardness of the mainly agrarian economies of the region, these exchanges remained provincial institutions. In 1927 they endeavored to strengthen their position by joining in the so-called Danubian Agreement with the grain exchange in Vienna, which was still stronger than these other exchanges. These efforts at cooperation collapsed almost immediately as one state after another introduced grain monopolies and stiff protective tariffs.

While Vienna historically was a significant international financial center, its importance as a capital market derived, above all, from its operations in Central and Southeastern Europe, including the Balkans. By the end of the nineteenth century, Vienna, as the financial capital of the Habsburg Empire, had reached a level of activity comparable to that of other advanced Western economic centers. Vienna, however, was distinguished from them by the crucial role played by its big banks and by the relative weakness of trade on its stock exchange. Indeed, both the Vienna and Budapest stock exchanges were periodically shaken by scandals, overheating, fraudulent speculation, corners, bubbles, and similar business practices including bribery of the press (not unknown in other financial centers)—in short, by activities that should have been controlled more effectively by legislation. Such state controls existed in Austria-Hungary and in Southeastern Europe, but were often ignored. The only interwar Central European state that kept a comparatively tight legislative grip on stock exchange dealings was Czechoslovakia. Consequently, the importance of stock exchanges as capital markets and as barometers of the national economies of Central and Southeastern Europe—at no time great—declined virtually to insignificance with the economic crisis of the early 1930s, and ceased altogether during World War II.

A Regional System of Bank Credit and Investment

Beginning in the second half of the nineteenth century, the Viennese banks played a special role in mobilizing capital, in channeling a substantial proportion of capital directly into industry, commerce, and insurance, and in acting as holding companies with diversified combines. In part, this role was a consequence of Austro-Hungarian legislation concerning incorporation and taxation, which unfavorably affected the growth of joint-stock and other forms of limited-liability enterprise and hindered the development of an adequate capital market.

Especially after the Vienna stock market crash of 1873, that city's banks tended to act in place of a capital market in promoting limited liability enterprises, converting firms into joint-stock companies, issuing shares, and providing long-term loans and generously renewable credit on current account to favored companies. Joint-stock companies as well as banks avoided the stock exchange, preferring to draw, if possible, on their own resources and take short-term bank credit. The latter they would eventually repay with new shares issued either by themselves or by banks on behalf of their client companies.

Because of the inadequacy of the capital market, banks secured their credits by acquiring controlling shareholdings in the largest and soundest undertakings and cementing their supervision of them by means of interlocking directorships. In Central and Southeastern Europe, the Austrian banking system performed the usual functions of accumulating and mobilizing capital, as it did in other developed countries, but it also played a much more active role in capital utilization. By virtue of their controlling interest in firms they had converted into large joint-stock companies, the Viennese banks became a primary force in the furthering of oligopolistic business organizations after the turn of the century. The banks initiated or mediated mergers and, probably to a greater extent than elsewhere, encouraged cartelization. They often took over marketing functions for enterprises in their sphere of interest by establishing sales departments, or they acted as cartel bureaus for whole branches of industry, such as sugar, coal, and wood. Company law and tax legislation encouraged the linking of the banking system and industrial and commercial enterprises so that the large commercial banks were at the same time substituting for a money market. All this tended to limit competition by internalizing market functions generally.

By the eve of World War I, eight great Viennese banks held about two-thirds of the total capital of all financial institutions of the Habsburg Empire; they also had secured strategic positions in almost all branches of industry. Numerous industrial and commercial enterprises clustered around the big banks, tied to them either by direct investments or by credits. In this way the large joint-stock banks had thrown a net of relationships with varying degrees of dependency over virtually every field of production and trade, and reached from Vienna to all territories of the former Habsburg Monarchy and the Balkans. In the Hungarian part of the Dual Monarchy only one bank, the Hungarian General Credit Bank, could be compared to the leading Vienna banks, and it was linked to the Austrian Creditanstalt für Handel und Gewerbe, Vienna's largest bank. In the industrially advanced Czech lands (Bohemia, Moravia, and Silesia), it was the Živnostenska Banka which spread its influence among Czech enterprises, as well as among enterprises in the Slavic areas of Southeastern Europe, reaching the height of its development as a universal bank during the first Czechoslovak Republic (1918–38). The big commercial banks in Austria, Czechoslovakia, and Hungary intervened on the Vienna, Prague, and Budapest stock exchanges. For instance, they influenced the exchange value of securities, offering more for sale if there was potential demand or withdrawing their shares or buying more if demand fell too low.

The system described above shaped the evolution of financial and capital relations in the successor states of Central and Southeastern Europe during the interwar period. Parallel developments in the financial and banking structures of other countries, Austria, Czechoslovakia, Hungary, Poland, Italy, Romania, Yugoslavia, and Bulgaria, continued after the dissolution of the Habsburg Monarchy.

The common features of the system can be summarized as follows: The universal banks of Vienna, Prague, and Budapest remained the traditional sources of finance for business enterprises throughout the region. Deposits were largely insufficient, and toward the end of the 1920s they decreased further. The banks borrowed heavily abroad, mainly on a short-term basis, channeling funds to their business clientele in their own countries as well as in Southeastern Europe. In addition, the large industrial companies frequently bypassed the banks and the stock market at home and took up credits either from foreign banks directly or through issues on the New York or London markets on their behalf. The big Viennese banks faced perennial liquidity problems, and concentration in the banking sector through mergers intensified. By 1934 only one big bank, the Creditanstalt, remained on the scene.

The former financial center of the Danubian Basin, Vienna was dramatically affected by the disintegration of the Habsburg Empire. Nevertheless, the Viennese commercial banks tried to carry on business as usual. They could operate as long as they had access to international finance either through substantial foreign participation in their equity or through comparatively large hard-currency accounts that leading Western banks held at the big Viennese commercial banks through Western loans. Expecting to recover their financial leadership in Central and Southeastern Europe, the Viennese commercial banks continued to credit not only their Austrian clients, but also enterprises throughout the former Habsburg Empire. By the mid-1920s, however, most of their branches and many of their subsidiary enterprises had been severed from them through the policy of nostrification (the transfer to domestic ownership) in the successor states, which involved the transfer of company headquarters to new states. Most important, the Viennese banks lost control over their most profitable affiliates and industrial enterprises in Czechoslovakia, where substantial assets and some of their most important clients successively were transferred to Czech banks, in particular to the Živnostenská Banka. Vienna was unable to regain its status as the undisputed financial center of Central and Southeastern Europe, that role having been irretrievably lost to New York, London, and Paris.

While Vienna was still serving as a mediator, international investors throughout Central and Southeastern Europe were being officially encouraged to participate in the equity of the leading banks and thus to penetrate the network of links between banks and industrial and trading enterprises, such as the Hungarian General Credit Bank in Budapest, the Bank Handlowy in Warsaw, the Banca Marmorosch, Blank and Co. in Bucharest, and the Bulgarian General Credit Bank in Sofia. Among the largest joint-stock banks in the capital cities of Central and Southeastern Europe, the Živnostenska Banka in Prague was a conspicuous exception. Without any foreign capital of its own, it invested through shareholdings, often together with Western business groups in Southeast European banking and industry. Mainly in this manner—and only sparingly through stock exchange operations—channels were kept open through which industry and commerce could be reached. It was through the universal banks of Central Europe that the creditor economies continued to use financial flows similar to the pre-1914 investment patterns in Austria-Hungary and Russia.

Western Investment and Its Limits

Some observers assumed that Central and Southeastern Europe region were economically paralyzed by enormous war losses and the breakup of the Austro-Hungarian Empire, and thus held little attraction for prospective investors from the Western democracies. Urgent pleas for aid from the new governments of the successor states met with little response. Few public loans were extended. Yet there existed objective economic and specific political conditions that were more conducive to the participation of foreign capital in the Danubian region than was supposed.

The period from 1919 to 1924 was decisive for changes in the structure and importance of international investments in interwar Central and Southeastern Europe. Instead of the traditional prewar state loans, influential financial and business groups from the Western democracies, strongly encouraged by the successor governments, acquired direct shares in the joint-stock capital of the largest commercial banks and industrial companies of the new states. International investment, so coveted by the capital-starved successor states, reached an interwar peak in 1930. After that the world economic crisis halted investment and the amount fell somewhat. No striking structural changes in the distribution of direct, long-term, participating investment occurred until after the *Anschluß* of Austria in March 1938 and the Munich agreement of September 1938, which was followed by the dismemberment of Czechoslovakia.

At the beginning of the interwar period, Western investment gained a priority which was maintained until the eve of World War II, amounting to 75 percent of total direct investment. (This included investment from Britain, France, the United States, Belgium, Holland, and Switzerland, and did not include German investment.) Britain and France took either first or second place in the order of international investors, while Germany, the leader before 1914, held fifth or sixth place on average.

The total amount of foreign investment in individual economies varied from country to country, but its composition in

Central and Southeastern Europe profoundly influenced industrial structure and performance. The different levels of foreign investment can be illustrated by comparing foreign public loans to direct foreign participating investment as a percentage of total public indebtedness and total capital of six countries in the region. If percentages are compared, it becomes obvious that foreign capital had a much stronger hold over industry and banking in the predominantly agrarian economies than it did over those sectors of the industrially more advanced economies of Czechoslovakia and Hungary. Disaggregation of the total distribution of foreign investment among the branches of industry reveals an identical pattern in all these economies: The highest proportion of foreign shares was found in mining and metallurgy, followed by chemicals, engineering, stone, glass, ceramics, wood, textiles, paper, and printing.

How did the influx of foreign investment encouraged by the capital-seeking interwar East European states affect economic and—particularly—industrial development? First, foreign capital was usually concentrated in the extraction and capital goods industries. For example, in Poland over 70 percent, in Czechoslovakia over 60 percent, and in Yugoslavia over 80 percent of total foreign capital was invested in mining and metallurgy. In Romania over 90 percent of foreign capital was invested in the oil industry. Second, foreign capital almost invariably participated in the more concentrated section of each branch of industry, that is, in the minority of joint-stock companies in which the majority of the industry's capital and productive capacity was concentrated. Third, by flowing into the strongest and largely already concentrated industries, or by initiating or taking part in establishing large combinations, direct foreign investment emphasized and accelerated tendencies toward large-scale enterprises in the receiving economies. Fourth, foreign capital was invested mostly in those branches of industry that were interwoven with the international business interests of the investors, and, although it played a positive role in encouraging industrialization, the investment was directed to serving the interests of the capital-exporting economies rather than those of the receiving countries. This practice created islands of comparatively advanced industrial complexes in a sea of dwarf enterprises which continued to perform an important economic function on the home markets in all pre-World War II East European countries.

To receive foreign loans, the successor states had to be integrated into the world currency system and thus into international finance and trade. Their currencies had to be stabilized and arrangements for the repayment of prewar and war loans had to be made. The successor states also linked their national banks to London, New York, and Paris, replacing previous links to Vienna and Paris. Efforts to restore the prewar credit mechanism were, however, doomed. Instead of a single gold standard, the Central and Southeast European governments were faced with a gold exchange standard driven by London and Washington, whose rates often differed. Interest rates, because of the greater risks involved, were high (7.5–8.0 percent versus the prewar 3.5–4.0 percent), prices received for loans were low (80–99 percent of nominal totals), and guarantees demanded by lenders were burdensome. The interest rates for long-term bank credits to industrial enterprises in Central and Southeastern Europe, however, varied between 15 and 30 percent from the mid-1920s into the 1930s.

Most foreign lending to Central and Southeastern Europe was limited to a comparatively short period that began with the League of Nations stabilization loans of 1922–28, which were joined by a flood of credits between 1924 and 1928. This stream dried up with the world economic crisis. From 1929 to 1933, capital imports slowed to a trickle, and by 1934–38 they had on balance changed into an outflow of sorely needed resources from the countries of the region.

At the peak of European interwar indebtedness (1931–32), half of the total external debt of the six Central and Southeast European countries consisted of pre-1918 loans. These included prewar debts of the Habsburg Monarchy and of the prewar regimes of Romania, Yugoslavia, and Bulgaria, as well as debts contracted during the war. To this were added commitments arising out of peace treaties, reparations from the defeated countries of Hungary and Bulgaria, and a "liberation contribution" from Czechoslovakia, Poland, Romania, and Yugoslavia to the Allied states. During the 1930s, total foreign indebtedness declined somewhat because of repayments, the devaluation of the creditor countries' currencies, and the reduction of interest rates. Yet the capital starvation of the region continued because at the same time that capital was withdrawn from the Central and Southeast European countries, no substantial new credits were forthcoming.

After 1929 international capital movements practically ceased to contribute to the domestic resources of the Central and Southeast European countries. Where there had been a marginal surplus, or at least a state of equilibrium before 1929, outgoing interest and dividend payments exceeded capital inflows in subsequent years, and starting in 1932 capital moved out altogether from all these countries. None was able to cover outflows with export surpluses, except Czechoslovakia, which still had to reduce capital exports simultaneously. Although massive state intervention, particularly exchange controls and strict foreign trade regulations, did lead to export surpluses, these proved insufficient to satisfy capital claims and commitments for interest and dividend payments.

Under prevailing political conditions in the Central and Southeast European countries, which, except for Czechoslovakia, had authoritarian governments, very little investment capital was imported. More than three-fourths of all the foreign loans contracted in the interwar period were used to cover budget deficits, consumption uses, and prestige spending, including excessive military expenditure, or to convert old debts repeatedly into new ones. Perhaps the most positive feature of East European public borrowing was that, on the one hand, some part of these loans was used for infrastructure and, on the other hand, some funds used for state expenditure trickled into industry. Such investment, however, did not absorb the major part of interwar loans. Basically, the input of capital, whether in the form of direct participation of foreign capital in industry or imports of foreign loans, was insufficient to generate sustained economic growth or to provide a viable domestic and export market for any of the countries of Central and Southeastern Europe in the long run.

Conclusion

Seen in historical context, the capital market in interwar Central and Southeastern Europe failed to engender capital accumulation or to support sustained economic growth. The results of empirical research into the economic and business history of Central and Southeastern Europe make it difficult to support the currently popular view that we must return to the democratic governments and free market economies of 1938. By then, with the exception of Czechoslovakia, there was hardly a shadow of democracy left anywhere in Central and Southeastern Europe; nor did a free-market economy exist anywhere by that time, including Czechoslovakia. As in other European countries, strict exchange controls and protectionist measures had been introduced after the world economic crisis that began in the early thirties. If a lesson is to be learned from the functioning of the region's interwar capital market, it would more likely be what to avoid rather than what to emulate.

Chapter 2

Current Capital Markets
in the United States, Western Europe,
and Japan

Maurice E. May

Capital markets are the decentralized planners of capitalist economic systems. Every day they are in the middle of an infinite number of buy/sell decisions. These markets are in constant motion, adjusting prices to reflect these decisions, and in the process allocating cheap capital to the worthy, and more expensive capital—or no capital at all—to the less worthy. These decisions are largely economic ones made by sellers, brokers, and buyers. In the primary markets, sellers, be they governments or corporations, sell stocks, bonds, or money-market securities to those middlemen (the underwriting brokers) who offer the best price. Buyers, be they households, institutions, or other governments or corporations, have money to invest from savings. In the secondary market, previously issued securities are resold to new investors.

While Western capital markets are free markets, governments play an important role in them by directly regulating underwriting and trading practices. Governments also play an indirect, often manipulative, role via monetary policy. Moreover, government fiscal policy has an impact, as does socially responsive tax policy. And in a democracy, voters influence many government policies.

For the most part, Western capital markets have adequate freedom to operate effectively for the benefit of their respective national economies, as well as the flexibility to evolve so as to meet new financial challenges. Governments can be overly restrictive of their capital markets, yet an ongoing debate over the proper balance between regulation and freedom in the market-government relationship is both necessary and healthy.

Capital markets consist of three major segments: equity (stock) markets, bond markets, and money markets. Equity markets include common and preferred stocks, bond markets government and corporate debt, and money markets short-term debt securities (both government and corporate) with maturities of less than one year. The emphasis in this chapter is on equity markets, with less attention paid to fixed-income markets.

This chapter provides a survey of the four largest securities markets in the world today: New York, Tokyo, London, and Frankfurt. Although they all include the same basic players—that is, government and corporate issuers, broker intermediaries, and household, institutional, and corporate ownership—each of these markets is different in its own way, for each is shaped by its own unique history.

The Four Major Capital Markets Today

In terms of size alone, the New York capital market is the world's biggest. Its fixed-income market is much larger than its nearest competitor, while its stock market is slightly ahead of Tokyo, with the gap widening as Tokyo weakens. As Table 2.1 indicates, the market capitalization (shortened in this chapter to *market cap*) of the three American exchanges is the largest in the world.[1] This is no surprise as the economy of the United States is also the world's largest.

The market cap of the Tokyo Stock Exchange does not lag far behind that of the American exchange, despite the Japanese gross national product (GNP) being only 57 percent of that of the United States (in dollars). In fact, the market cap of the Tokyo exchange surpassed that of the American exchanges for the period 1987–90. History plays a role here. Speculation by Japanese stock market participants coupled with the ability of "the club" of government and business leaders to manipulate absolute price levels, plus a lack of grounding in fundamental stock valuation, allowed Tokyo to rise during the 1980s to astronomical heights. But like all speculative market bubbles, this one also burst, starting early in 1990. Since then, the Tokyo Stock Exchange has suf-

TABLE 2.1
SIZE AND IMPORTANCE OF STOCK MARKETS

	12/31/90 Mkt. cap Local Currency (billions)	12/31/90 Mkt. cap US$billions	1990 GNP Local Currency (billions)	1990 GNP US$billions	Capitalization as percent of GNP
United States	$3,090	$3,090	$5,527	$5,527	55.9
New York Stock Exchange	2,692				
American Stock Exchange	75				
NASDAQ	323				
Japan (Tokyo)	Y 379,230	$2,797	Y 431,004	$3,179	88.0
1st Section	365,154				
2nd Section	14,076				
Great Britain					
London Stock Exchange	£460	$ 893	£562	$1,901	81.9
Germany	DM 510	$ 342	DM 2,492	$1,672	20.4
Official Market	488				
Regulated Market	11				
Free Market	11				

	US$	Yen	DM	Pound
US$	—	$0.0074	$0.67	$1.93
Yen	Y 135.4	—	Y 90.8	Y 261.8
DM	DM 1.49	DM 0.011	—	DM 2.88
£	£0.518	£0.0038	£0.347	—

SOURCES: American stock market data: the 1991 *Fact Books* of the New York and American Stock Exchanges, and of NASDAQ. Japan: the 1991 *Fact Book* of the Tokyo Stock Exchange. United Kingdom: the *Quality of Markets Quarterly Review,* winter edition, October-December 1990. Germany: "Stock Exchange Statistics 1990," published by the Frankfurter Wertpapierbörse, AG.

GNP data are for the fourth quarter 1990, annualized, except for Japan, which is for the third quarter 1990, annualized. Data source: "International Financial Statistics," published by the International Monetary Fund, July 1991, vol. 44, no. 7.

Exchange rates are from *The Wall Street Journal* (quoting Telerate), January 2, 1991, p. C10. The rates used throughout this chapter are as follows:

fered an orderly but dramatic and ongoing decline. Moreover, if New York, London, and Frankfurt valuations have implications for Tokyo, the Japanese exchange has much further to drop. (Japanese market valuations, in terms of price/earnings ratios, are discussed in greater detail below.)

In third and fourth place, respectively, are the market caps of Britain and Germany. This is initially surprising, given that the German economy is considerably larger—some 53 percent larger in U.S. dollars—than that of Britain. But history again plays a part. The dominant role of the German banks has prevented the normal evolution of the Frankfurt Stock Exchange, at least since World War I. Also, the Germans have privatized only sparingly, keeping nearly all utilities under the control of various federal and state government entities. The 1990 unification with the *Länder* of the former German Democratic Republic increased GNP somewhat, but so far has added not one pfennig to the market cap. As a result, the exchange's role in Germany is relatively smaller than its role in the three other countries discussed in this chapter.

Britain stands in sharp contrast to the countries of the other three major markets. British banks never blocked the normal evolution of the stock exchange; moreover, measures taken by the Thatcher government reinvigorated the old London Stock Exchange. The arrival of dealer-based trading and negotiated commissions in 1986 encouraged a competitive interest in capturing trading activity in foreign stocks. The privatization of thirty-six government-owned industrial and utility corporations over the past decade added meaningfully to the market cap of listed domestic shares: A total of £44.5 billion of market cap—almost 10 percent of the entire domestic listings of the exchange—has been created as a direct result of privatization. This infusion is likely to continue to increase, given that outstanding installments of electric distribution shares, as well as initial offerings of power generation shares, were not included in the market cap at the end of 1990. Moreover, a huge, second tranche of British Telecom shares was planned for November 1991.

Table 2.2 shows the value of shares traded on the major capital markets during 1990. Not surprising is the size of the New York and Tokyo turnover value. Table 2.2 also illustrates how overwhelmingly domestic are the New York, Frankfurt, and Tokyo stock markets in the value of their 1990 turnover. In contrast, the London market lives up to its official name, the "International

Stock Exchange." The domesticity of the Frankfurt and Tokyo markets can be partially explained by the continuation of fixed commission sales, while New York's domestic orientation is explained by the relatively strict American disclosure requirements. With its traditionally looser disclosure requirements and abandonment of fixed rate commissions in 1986, London has been able to capture significant business in foreign stocks. As Table 2.2 demonstrates, 48.2 percent of 1990 turnover value was in non-British stocks. London has been particularly successful in attracting business in German shares. It traded some £35 billion (the reported £70 billion halved) in German stocks in 1990, which represented 21.7 percent of London's foreign total.[2] Perhaps more illustrative is the fact that this figure amounts to DM 87 billion, versus DM 1,085 billion in Germany's total turnover value in domestic stocks, an 8-percent increment lost largely because of a noncompetitive commissions structure.

TABLE 2.2
1990 TURNOVER (VOLUME) ON MAJOR STOCK EXCHANGES

	Total turnover (billions)	Domestic stocks (billions)	Foreign stocks (billions)	Percent foreign stocks	Total turnover US$ (billions)
United States	$1,589	$1,486	$95	6.0%	$1,589
New York Stock Exchange	1,325	1,244	81	6.1%	1,325
NASDAQ	226	212	14	6.3%	226
American Stock Exchange	38	N/A	N/A	N/A	38
Japan/Tokyo	Y 188,682	Y 186,666	Y 2,012	1.1%	$1,392
1st Section	176,310				
2nd Section	10,356				
Foreign Section	2,016				
U.K./London	£305	£158	£147	48.2%	$ 592
Germany/ Federation	DM 1,128	DM 1,085	DM 43	3.8%	$ 757

NOTE: Turnover values as reported by NASDAQ and London include both dealer purchases separately from dealer sales, resulting in double counting. To maintain consistency, their numbers have been halved in this table.
SOURCES: The *Fact Books* for the NYSE, ASE, NASDAQ, Tokyo, and Frankfurt. London data are from the Research Department, the International Stock Exchange, London. NYSE foreign stock trading data were taken from the exchange's foreign listing department.

In Tokyo, seven of the ten largest market capitals are bank stocks, which indicates banking concentration, asset quality, and banking prominence. By contrast, none of the top ten in New York are bank stocks. The situation in the United States results from the fragmentation of the banking industry, low banking quality (assets), and a lack of power attributable to historical resistance to bank concentration. Citicorp, the largest U.S. bank, would not even place in the world's top fifty in terms of market cap. German financial companies—two banks and two insurance companies—hold four of the top ten spots in Frankfurt. Like banks, insurance companies are strong cross-share owners of other German companies. Top-ranked Allianz owns 23 percent of ninth-ranked Dresdner Bank.[3]

On the New York Stock Exchange, the importance of the American consumer is clearly evident. Three of the largest companies in the New York top ten, Philip Morris, Coca-Cola, and Procter & Gamble, manufacture only consumer products, while another top-ten company, Wal-Mart, retails them. Two others, Merck and Bristol-Myers Squibb, are giant pharmaceutical firms, selling products for individual consumption.

The Frankfurt exchange, in addition to its financial bias, is also committed to heavy industry. Two major chemical companies, Bayer and Hoechst, are represented in its top ten, along with a vehicle manufacturer, Daimler-Benz, and two diversified energy/power companies, VEBA and RWE.

The London exchange displays some of the fruits of British privatization, as two of its top five companies, British Telecom and British Gas, are products of the program. Otherwise, the London top ten is diversified among various industries and includes two conglomerates, Hanson and Grand Metropolitan.

One similarity shared by three of the four stock exchanges is the inclusion of a telephone company in their top tens: American Telephone & Telegraph (New York), Nippon Telephone and Telegraph (Tokyo), and British Telecom (London). The absence of a German equivalent is due to government ownership of the telephone network through the Deutsche Bundespost.

Degree of concentration illustrates a striking difference among the stock exchanges. In the two largest markets, New York and Tokyo, the top ten companies constitute just 15.4 and 16.1 percent, respectively, of market cap. For London and Frankfurt, the third and fourth largest markets, the ten largest stock companies make up 24.2 and 39.2 percent, respectively. Large companies clearly increase their dominance as markets get smaller.

Everything discussed so far relates to the secondary, or "after" market. This market is the most visible because of its size. It is absolutely crucial because it provides the opportunity for purchasers of initial public offerings to sell their stock. Without the secondary market, there would likely be no primary market. The primary market is where capital is raised. Savers accumulate capital while companies require capital to expand, and, consequently, a channel between the two is needed. Enter the middlemen, the so-called investment bankers, who work for brokerage firms with large sales capabilities. These bankers seek deals, that is, blocks of stock from companies that want to raise equity capital. They will buy blocks of stock from companies and then quickly attempt to resell them via their sales forces to savers. Risk is usually spread among many different underwriters with the formation of syndicates.

American underwriters dominate the international distribution of equities (defined as underwriter participation in equity outside their domestic markets). Five of the top ten underwriters in 1990 were American firms, while a sixth was a joint U.S. venture with Credit Suisse. Japan was poorly represented, although its largest brokerage firm, Nomura, placed a strong second. (One should note that in the 1989 rankings, two other Japanese firms, Daiwa and Yamaichi, joined Nomura in the top ten.) After the Americans and Japanese, international underwriting becomes scattered. Overall, the value of shares involved in international underwriting is small. Total volume for the top ten international underwriters amounts to just $7.3 billion; the volume of the top twenty-five is close to $10.1 billion. These numbers appear modest when compared to the value of outstanding market cap, and in comparison to debt issues.

The most basic valuation of stocks is the price-to-earnings, or P/E, ratio. This is derived by dividing a company's current stock price by its annual earnings per share. As the stock market tends to be a discounting mechanism which forecasts the future more than it reflects the past, securities analysts prefer to calculate their P/E ratios on forecasted earnings rather than on past, already reported, earnings. Other important measures of valuation include price to cash flow (usually income plus depreciation), price to book value per share, and current dividend yield.

The American, British, and German exchanges trade basically on the same valuations, as Table 2.3 shows. High bond yields in Britain mean that the market demands a higher yield from its shares. The relatively high German corporate tax rates lead to the "hiding" of earnings in reserve funds, so cash flow is high relative to earnings. Surprising numbers come out of Japan. Despite the existence of a downward trend in stock prices throughout 1991 that had been underway for more than a year, valuations remained out of line with those in the other major markets of the world.

TABLE 2.3
VALUATION MEASUREMENTS OF MAJOR MARKETS

	U.S.	Tokyo	London	Frankfurt
P/E Ratio	18.5x	42.9x	13.2x	12.0x
Price/Cash Flow	8.4x	15.5x	7.2x	2.9x
Price/Book Value	290%	300%	230%	130%
Dividend Yield	2.8%	0.8%	4.6%	2.8%

SOURCE: Goldman Sachs, "World Investment Strategy Highlights," April 1991, p. 1. Based on a sample of industrial companies in each country, priced as of April 2, 1991, using 1991 estimates.

P/E ratios remained extremely high, while corporate yields were held quite low by the lack of dividend payments. An American securities analyst would point to speculation to explain the high P/E ratio and to lack of shareholder power to explain the low dividends. Japanese analysts point to the high Japanese growth rate, higher corporate leverage, and stronger cash flows. It nonetheless seems reasonable to hope that Japanese share valuations will someday approximate those of the other major markets so that the Tokyo stock market will once again become attractive to foreign investors.

Impediments to Growth in Western Equity Markets

Relatively high fixed-rate commissions traditionally have been used by major exchanges with monopoly power to sustain revenues. The New York Stock Exchange, under government threat of abolition, switched from fixed to negotiable commissions on the famous "May Day," May 1, 1975. A decade later, the London Stock Exchange followed suit and negotiated commissions became part of an overall reform known as the "Big Bang" of October 27, 1986. The results of deregulation in both New York and London have been sharply falling commission rates (especially for the large institutional money managers who possess the clout to drive them down the most), and greater trading volume, which enhances market liquidity.

Frankfurt and Tokyo remain holdouts, maintaining fixed commissions. Frankfurt, however, has felt the pressure as London has captured a significant amount of international business in German blue-chip stocks. Because Frankfurt aspires to become a more important international financial center, the fixed rate of commissions has been lowered substantially and the onerous transfer tax has been abolished in the past two years.

London has the least stringent listing requirements in the world, and consequently does the greatest volume of international business. The United States regulatory requirement of full disclosure, which includes quarterly reports to the federal government, remains an ideal that the rest of the world might do well to emulate. Full disclosure is also required of foreign companies if they wish to have full listings on the New York Stock Exchange, a stipulation which restrains international trading in the United States.

Although the basic format of income statements and balance sheets is standard, generally accepted accounting principles vary from country to country. Britain uses current, replacement-cost accounting to value assets, while the United States uses historical cost. Goodwill (the premium price-over-book value paid for acquired companies) is immediately written off in Britain, whereas it must be slowly amortized in the United States, often over forty years. German companies can manipulate (or "smooth") earnings by booking "reserve" expenses during good times, which are available subsequently to come back into earnings during bad times. Japanese companies use accelerated depreciation on their income statements, while American, British, and German companies use straight-line depreciation, a practice which results in higher reported earnings. The international securities analyst must adjust any analysis in light of these various practices.

Prospects for Western Capital Markets

Significant changes appear to be underway in all four of the major capital markets. In New York, the American financial community faces bank consolidation, as well as mergers between brokerage houses and banks. While some Americans may feel nostalgic for a simpler era when "small was beautiful," the reality is that American financial institutions must consolidate in order to cope with an increasingly competitive domestic and international environment. Interstate and regional mergers among U.S. banks already are occurring. Legislation due for consideration in 1992 should make nationwide banking reform possible.

In Tokyo, "the club" is under pressure. Another market scandal—the second in three years—is likely to bring more than the usual "rolling heads" response from the Japanese government. Real reform in the form of negotiated commissions may be the price "the club" will have to pay to repair its reputation. Furthermore, the stock market has been in decline for more than a year, as its high valuations gradually come down to earth. These developments are painful for the Japanese, but in the long run they will help ease the integration of the Japanese capital markets with those of the rest of the world. Ironically, Nomura Securities may achieve its long-term goal of being more of a global securities house as a result of current developments.

Continued privatization coupled with competitive negotiated commissions and a dynamic dealer network bodes well for the London Stock Exchange (recently renamed the International Stock Exchange). Domestically, however, Britain faces a deep and lengthy recession as it brings its monetary policy into line with the highly disciplined policy of the European Community (EC) emerging after the Maastricht agreement.

Newly unified Germany has international aspirations for the Frankfurt Exchange. At the dedication of the renovated Frankfurt Stock Exchange building in April 1990, Finance Minister Theodor Waigel called for the Bundesbank to remain in Frankfurt in a unified Germany, and stated that the European central bank should be set up there as well. However, one obvious problem may check German ambitions: The small, tight membership of the inner club of the German financial circle is incompatible with Germany's aspirations for a continental, or even global, financial role. No one questions that Germany has done an excellent job of managing its economy or that the economic potential of a unified Germany surpasses that of the pre-1989 Federal Republic. The problem lies with the dynamics of Germany's financial community. Fixed commissions and insider trading are also issues. Will "the club" remain closed, or will it open up?

Lessons for the Capital Markets of Eastern Europe

The new democracies of Eastern Europe cannot wait for their capital markets to evolve. Revolutionary action by the new governments is required to privatize enterprises and organize capital markets. In addition, business activity must grow quickly. Perhaps yesterday's black marketeers and today's small merchants will become tomorrow's businesspeople, investors, stockbrokers, and traders.

Capital markets depend on capital formation, which, in turn, depends on savings. Economists emphasize the maxim that the marginal propensity to save increases as income increases. Consequently, small business proprietors must prosper if they are to become active in the stock market. It should be noted that New York merchants launched their stock exchange late in the eighteenth century, while rice traders and money changers established the Osaka Stock Exchange in the latter part of the nineteenth century. Small businesses in Eastern Europe are likely nongovernment sources of domestic capital.

Investment through Western capital markets in the new democracies of Eastern Europe is likely to be small. There are simply too many institutional barriers on both sides. Western stockbrokers and money managers follow established patterns of investment. For instance, Gardner & Preston Moss, Inc., of Boston, has approximately $2 billion in assets under management, split evenly between stocks and bonds, but it emphasizes conservative management. The stocks are blue chip, and the bonds are U.S. treasuries or high-quality corporates. There is no hope from this source, unfortunately: $2 billion, but not a penny for, say, Bulgaria.

Many international investors also seem locked into a mind-set which virtually precludes investment in Eastern Europe. For instance, one popular approach to international investing begins with the disaggregation of global market cap by country. Next, the investment merits of each country are considered, and the investment plan is then mapped out by overvaluing the market cap of attractive stock markets and devaluing that of less attractive ones. Emerging stock markets with virtually no market cap are thus eliminated.

On a more positive note, one investment, the East German Investment Trust, was organized by Ermgassen & Co., of London and Frankfurt, and underwritten in early 1991 by County NatWest and the Berliner Bank, AG. The sale of the issue raised £40 million (almost $80 million at the current exchange rate) for the purchase of companies from the Treuhandanstalt, the German agency charged with privatizing the eight thousand enterprises of the former German Democratic Republic. The issue initially was sold with some difficulty as a private placement to individuals of high net worth, but subsequently was listed on the London Exchange.[4] It may still be the only publicly traded vehicle of investment in Eastern Europe.

Batterymarch Financial Management of Boston currently is launching its Soviet Companies Fund to take positions in privatized, joint-stock companies from the former Soviet Union. The fund will neither be marketed through nor traded in the capital markets. Plans, however, exist for the introduction of ventures similar in purpose to the East German Investment Trust.[5]

Some potential for investment may exist with the so-called country funds, many of which are traded on the New York Stock Exchange. These are closed-end mutual-fund shares sold by brokerage firms in normal underwritings for investment in shares from a particular country. Their purpose is to make investment in emerging stock markets easier for participants in major capital markets. Some examples are the Taiwan Fund, the Mexico Fund, and the Brazil Fund. Before a country fund can be established, however, there must be an emerging stock market with a number of issues and some market capitalization.

While their best hope for the immediate future may lie in joint ventures with Western corporations, East European economies should make every effort to privatize as much as possible, sell shares to as many people as possible, and establish working stock exchanges. Whatever is done in the short run will provide a better springboard at a later date for large-scale mobilization of capital. Joint ventures and, as they develop, domestic companies will need at least some financing through domestic capital markets. If those markets are to grow, a bit of classic advice from American brokers may be instructive: "Stocks are sold, not bought." This means not waiting for the public to show up at bank windows to buy stock but instead going out and selling by whatever means it takes: advertisements, brokers on the telephone, installment plans, cartoon characters, and even specialized "share shops."

Notes

[1]NASDAQ (for "National Association of Securities Dealers Automated Quotations") is not an exchange per se, but rather an interactive computer system linking the trading rooms of more than four hundred brokerage firms. It is a dealer-based network in which brokers specify stocks in which they want to "make a market." Brokers maintain an inventory of these stocks, and their positions can either be positive ("long") or negative ("short").

[2]According to Steve Webster, Research Department, International Stock Exchange, London.

[3]"Allianz Profits Decline 9 Percent," *Financial Times*, July 31, 1991. The 23 percent ownership in Dresdner Bank was announced at the same time as first-half 1991 results.

[4]Per conversation with Walter Zinsser, Ermgassen & Co., August 9, 1991.

[5]Per conversation with Dean LeBaron, Batterymarch Financial Management, August 16, 1991.

Chapter 3

The Role of Foreign Investment in East European Privatization: Hungary, Poland, and Czechoslovakia

Dirk W. Damrau

The inflated expectations of massive private foreign investment in Eastern Europe have collapsed as rapidly as the euphoria surrounding the initial political transformations in each of the region's countries. Although the three countries of East Central Europe, Hungary, Poland, and Czechoslovakia, were thought to have the best chances of surmounting the challenges posed by four decades of stifling bureaucratic planning, distorted trade relations, and macroeconomic disequilibrium, the progress toward privatization of the overwhelmingly state-owned and state-controlled economies of these nations has been painfully slow, and the participation of Western private capital has been no more than modest. This observation is not intended to minimize the progress that has been made in all these countries toward economic stabilization, redirection of trade toward the West (in some cases accompanied by current account surpluses), and institutionalization of liberal democratic political practice; however, little doubt exists that all three countries will have to make more serious efforts to include private foreign capital in their transformation plans if they are truly intent on creating "normal" free-market–dominated economies. Their success at soliciting official assistance, either through official bilateral sources or via the multilateral institutions for development, has been impressive—the three countries combined will see inflows of at least US$10 billion in 1991. Although these inflows are necessary to much-needed investments in public infrastructure and will complement private foreign capital investment, there is no example of a successfully developing country in which official capital inflows were dominant in the initiation of rapid economic growth. The principal argument of this chapter is that foreign inflows of private capital are necessary and indeed indispensable to the creation of advanced, industrialized free-market–oriented economies in Eastern Europe.

Foreign Investment, Real and Presumed

The amount of space devoted to East European investments in international financial publications belies the region's meager success at actually attracting voluntary foreign investment. Although the real numbers are no reflection of Eastern Europe's true investment potential, and it is admittedly too early to begin comparing the region to areas where market economies are well-established, the low total so far underscores the fact that the East European economies will have to be much more aggressive in identifying areas of comparative advantage and courting foreign investment if they are to represent anything more than relatively impoverished and modest extensions of the enormous West European market to foreign investors. The competition for capital is increasingly international and there is no reason to assume that Eastern Europe's location alone is enough to make it attractive to foreign investors. As countries such as India, Argentina, and the republics of the former Soviet Union emerge into global capital flows, the East European countries will have to move more quickly just to keep up. This is particularly true in relations with North American and East Asian investors who have not yet generally discerned a comparative advantage in Eastern Europe. Table 3.1 compares the three countries of East Central Europe to the most attractive direct and portfolio investment destinations in the developing world on the basis of the magnitude of private foreign capital inflows.[1]

The Political Paradox of Asset Pricing

Politicians in East Central Europe and their economic managers are facing a contradiction between the obvious need for foreign

TABLE 3.1
PRIVATE FOREIGN CAPITAL INFLOWS, 1991 ESTIMATES

| | *(figures in US$ millions)* | |
	Direct and portfolio equity investment	Commercial bank lending (net)
East Central Europe[a]	$ 1,400	Negligible[b]
Latin America[c]	20,400	$15,700[d]
Malaysia	3,800	1,000
Thailand	2,200	7,200
Indonesia	1,400	2,000
Portugal	3,500	2,500
Turkey	3,400	1,000

SOURCE: Institute of International Finance and Salomon Brothers, Inc., estimates.
[a]Czechoslovakia, Hungary, and Poland.
[b]Hungary and Czechoslovakia issued US$1.27 billion in bonds in 1991. A large portion was placed with commercial banks, essentially exchanged for syndicated loans which are not being refinanced.
[c]See Salomon Brothers, Inc., "Private Capital Flows to Latin America: Volume Triples to US$40 Billion," February 1992.
[d]This includes a significant number of new public-sector or private corporate international bond issues being placed with nonbank investors.

capital in the privatization process and popular discontent with the prospect of exchanging domestic communist control for foreign control. In none of the emerging democracies of Eastern Europe is there a significant constituency advocating aggressive foreign investment in the domestic economy. Every government in the region has had to deal with political pressure to prevent foreigners (in some instances a specific nationality) from buying up domestic entities "on the cheap." Such accusations have emerged at a time when the new governments are loathe to alienate any sector of the electorate. The new administrators find it difficult to explain to the public that it would be difficult to *give* many treasured enterprises of the communist era to foreign investors, much less to ask these potential investors to pay exorbitant amounts in convertible currency for minority stakes. It is not surprising that workers brought up in a communist socialist system fail to appreciate the value of capital (read foreign capital, since domestic capital is extremely limited) and managerial expertise.

The discrepancy between value as determined by potential foreign investors and value as perceived by the public or as calculated by deposed central planners poses major challenges to to the new democratic politicians, as well as to the accountants, consultants, and merchant bankers who are attempting to combat the legacy of central planning. The much-touted Polish and Czechoslovak voucher systems have been devised as much to give the general population the *impression* that it has a stake in the disposition of its country's corporate holdings and thus to deflect popular concern with foreign investment, as to accelerate privatization.

The Problem of Control

The political paradox confronting would-be foreign investors is closely related to the desire of these investors to retain control over their prospective stake in East Central Europe. Although most potential investments in the region call for venture capital, there are few foreign investors willing to relinquish either management or ownership. (There are exceptions to this generalization. Strategic investors attempting to tap into a domestic franchise, for example in retailing or commercial banking, or investors in a clearly profitable ongoing operation, may be willing to take minority shares.)

Yet some who favor privatization see only a limited role for foreign investors. Certain aspects of the voucher system take the discontinuity between control and new capital's contribution to an extreme. Minority foreign investors will contribute virtually all of the new capital, managerial expertise, and technological modernization essential in many cases if the enterprise is to survive in a competitive market, while the majority equity holders (retained state holdings, employee or management owners, and the general public) will have no obligation to contribute new capital to the survival of the enterprise. This discontinuity will end only when equity markets are fully operational and integrated into international capital markets, and foreign investment cannot be put off for that long. Most prominent investments in the region have included provisions for substantial Western investor control over the enterprise.

Few outside investors will be enthusiastic about investing capital in an enterprise in which workers, former managers, and the state retain majority stakes. Worker self-management in the region has been characterized more by short-term income maximization than by serious interest in the enterprise's long-term economic viability. State ownership will be subject to political concern with employment (primarily avoiding mass redundancy). Although adept at bargaining for scarce inputs in the old centrally planned system, enterprise managers in the region are untested in free-market environments. These managers are not natural majority partners for a typical Western investor.

The reluctance to permit outright foreign ownership of land, symptomatic of the general ambivalence toward foreign investment, is another potential obstacle to such investment. Although limitations on foreign residential or farm property ownership are not unusual in developing countries, they are less common in advanced industrialized countries. In combination with uncertainty over true ownership and potential restitution of property, these limitations may impede foreign participation. Although long-term leases on land are common in places such as Britain or Hong Kong, they are less acceptable to most North American and Asian investors. Furthermore, there are understandable historical reasons why foreign ownership of property might pose political problems, for example German acquisition of land in western Poland. Yet such hesitations could also restrict the flow of natural direct foreign investment.

Restitution and the Confusion over Property Rights

The claims of former property owners or their descendants on companies, shops, and land being denationalized throughout Eastern Europe are a significant source of uncertainty for private and potential investors, both domestic and foreign. Restitution creates a potentially overwhelming financial liability to governments already confronting serious fiscal deficits. The new democratic governments must balance political pressure to repudiate past arbitrary confiscations, particularly during the first decade of communist rule, with the real desire to speed up the privatization process and reassure private investors that they have a secure claim on the property they purchase. An additional complication emerges from the fact that many of the former owners of confiscated property, now residents abroad, could be a significant source of new investment, and therefore should not be alienated.

The three countries of East Central Europe have begun tackling restitution at different speeds. Czechoslovakia and Hungary set deadlines by which claims on property had to be lodged with the authorities. Although sorting out the legitimacy of these claims will be a time-consuming process and a bureaucratic nightmare, as it has been in the five *Länder* of eastern Germany, at least potential investors will have some hint in the near future of potential legal entanglements. Hungary has gone even further, essentially denying compensation in kind except in specific cases of agricultural land which will actually be farmed by its owners. The Hungarian government hopes to avoid potentially huge costs by limiting compensation and giving the former owners privatization vouchers or bonds rather than cash.

Polish authorities, in contrast, have only begun considering restitution. Passage of general legislation covering the legality of claims for the return of property was postponed until after the October 27, 1991, elections, as repatriation had become a source of conflict between President Lech Wałęsa and then-Prime Minister Tadeuz Mazowiecki. No significant progress has since been made.

The Region's Comparative Advantage

It is still not obvious to many international investors why East Central Europe might be a viable venue for foreign investment. The argument that the region might provide access to the promising post-Soviet market has become hollow as the republics of the former Soviet Union approach insolvency, and as trade collapses between them and Eastern Europe. Linguistic talents, geographic ties, and four decades of experience in dealing with Soviet partners may eventually be advantages to a Western investor, but these advantages cannot be even vaguely quantified until the situation in the post-Soviet republics stabilizes. The revolution underway in the former Soviet Union, in combination with that region's much cheaper labor costs and proximate natural resources, may obviate the need to invest in Eastern Europe to gain access to the post-Soviet market. The Central European rush toward Western Europe also makes the advantages of Eastern ties less evident.

Even more significant, the potential of East Central Europe as a source of inexpensive but talented labor for Western investors supplying Western Europe has diminished over the past year. The costs of establishing a new operation in Warsaw or Prague—

finding office space, hiring an experienced, multilingual staff, securing legal and accounting expertise, and installing telephone connections—are as high as in major West European cities, and the process is considerably more time-consuming. This is probably not the case for investors in manufacturing or processing outside the major cities, but the threat that the wage productivity gap could increase rapidly and cause financial disaster, as it has in the eastern *Länder* of Germany, haunts many potential investors lured by the prospect of cheap labor. Disproportionately high wage expectations could also diminish the region's attractiveness. Turkey, Mexico, Thailand, Malaysia, and possibly the Balkans, as well as the former Soviet republics, could provide cheaper labor of comparable productivity.

Finally, the potential of domestic demand is still far from fulfilled. Only Poland, with its thirty-eight million people, provides a potentially large domestic market. The persistent—albeit temporary—depression affecting the region, however, does not instill confidence. Ironically, emerging friction between the three countries in reestablishing commercial relations with each other and the promise of ties to the European Community makes the case for a secure regional or even domestic market for direct foreign investment less compelling.

Currency Inconvertibility

The three countries of East Central Europe have moved further on the issue of currency convertibility and the related technical ability to repatriate profits than on many other problems facing potential Western investors. All three countries have established provisions for foreign investors to remit profits earned in domestic currency in convertible currencies. Poland has extremely liberal currency regulations, and Hungary has virtually established the convertibility of the forint. Although the three countries are still some distance from convertibility for capital account transactions (many West European countries have only recently established capital account convertibility), progress on current account convertibility has been impressive. Although foreign investors still face the risk of dealing in currencies beset by relatively high inflation (and resultant depreciation or devaluation), rapid moves to liberalize domestic prices have made these risks relatively calculable.

The Lingering Perception of Bankruptcy

All the economies of Eastern Europe suffer from the perception that huge external debts incurred by the previous regimes make them particularly bad risks. This perception is reflected in the fact that syndicated commercial bank lending to the region, the traditional source of external finance, has become insignificant. In 1990, Western commercial banks withdrew an estimated net US$15 billion from the technically solvent countries of Eastern Europe (including the Soviet Union). In some respects, the perception of de facto insolvency is justified. Poland and Bulgaria have defaulted on most of their external debt, which has put them in bad stead with their commercial bank creditors. Major Western commercial banks will obviously not be optimistic when queried by their corporate clients on opportunities in these two countries. Many entities in the Soviet Union effectively defaulted on trade credits and other short-term debt contracted in the past two years because commercial relationships were decentralized. The former Soviet republics are in the midst of a liquidity crisis that will likely lead to a full-scale restructuring of the USSR's external debt among the components of the Commonwealth of Independent States. Albania may be one of the few countries in the world which has managed to default on its spot currency transactions.

There are exceptions to the perception of high risk. Czechoslovakia's communist regime pursued an extremely conservative approach to taking on external debt. This has left the new democratic government with a good credit standing and considerable flexibility in new borrowing on international capital markets. Despite the cliché about Hungary having the highest per-capita debt in Eastern Europe, the Hungarian government has pursued a steadfast policy of servicing its US$21.3 billion external debt.[2] It is no coincidence that Hungary has maintained an impeccable record of willingness to meet its obligations, and that it is by far the main destination of direct foreign investment in Eastern Europe.

The worst case of debt management in East Central Europe obviously is Poland, which defaulted on its long-term commercial bank debt in December 1989. Poland achieved an extraordinary 50-percent forgiveness of its debt from the Paris Club of official creditors in March 1991. An eventual resolution along the lines of the Brady Plan, put forward by the U.S. secretary of the treasury, currently is being negotiated with commercial bank (London Club) creditors. The negotiations have not been easy. Although private debt amounted to only 25 percent of Poland's total external debt, the manner in which the country's private obligations are resolved will shape future perceptions of Poland's creditworthiness. An ambitious and extensive debt-for-equity or asset scheme with a Brady Plan resolution, although politically difficult domestically, would serve the dual purpose of limiting the long-term damage to relations with Western commercial banks and motivating the banks to find clients who want to invest in Poland.

Restricted Sources of Credit

The perceived international insolvency of the East European countries is matched by the disastrous condition of domestic commercial credit. Under central planning, banks served as conduits of scarce capital, not according to any rational calculation of economic viability, but on the bases of political connections and influence. Commercial banks in some countries were either bastions of communist party patronage or warehouses for personnel who could play no other role in the centrally managed system of production. The commercial banks ("dispensers of preallocated public funds" would be a more appropriate term) were hostages to their client authorities, whether through ownership, political connections, or inertia. Over the years of central planning, the commercial banks essentially were forced to give out loans to cover the accumulated losses of the corporate sector, which means that they have inherited portfolios of bad loans.

Although structural, legal, and partial personnel changes have taken place in most of the banks, little has actually been done to create a viable commercial banking system. The banks' burden of bad corporate debt has severely limited their ability or willingness to extend new credit and to provide a viable domestic source of capital. Public financial concerns have made governments hesitant or unwilling to assume or guarantee bad corporate debts, as has been done in eastern Germany. Foreign ownership and establishment of banks is paradoxically limited. Most of the countries have inherited a no-win situation from their former governments in which domestic entrepreneurs, foreign investors, and privatized enterprises are starved for domestic currency credit, while outside involvement in the sector is severely limited and new domestic entrants are stifled by the franchises inherited from the old regime. The creation of a viable commercial banking system is one of the most pressing challenges facing the new governments, although progress on this front has dangerously slowed economic stabilization. If as much international publicity were focused on the reform of domestic commercial credit markets as is put on stock-market openings, the process might have proceeded more quickly. The World Bank has at least been constructive in providing loans for the reform of the banking sector.

Significant Portfolio Investment Not in Sight

Despite the international attention focused on the opening of stock exchanges in Warsaw and Budapest, it will be a considerable time before portfolio investment becomes a major vehicle for foreign investment in Eastern Europe. The exceptions are the listings of the best regional corporations on Western stock exchanges and investment undertaken indirectly through the growing number of Western-managed investment funds directed at the region. Inconvertible currencies, the limited pool of private domestic savings, continued economic depression, technical problems in distribution, the mixed performance of the first issues, and problems facing the commercial banking sector have impeded the rapid emergence of viable equity markets. The recent initial public offering by a furniture company in Poland has provided a promising second start to the process of privatization via initial public offerings there, but also underscores the reality that such offerings will be cautiously implemented and will be the exception rather than the rule in the overall privatization process over the near term.

Problems with Valuation

Major problems in evaluating the value of potential investment in East Central Europe are integrally related to the political challenges outlined above. Although asset valuation and the implementation of new accounting policies and privatization strategies have been a boon to Western consultants, accountants, and anyone else receiving subsidies through the British Know-How Fund, they remain a costly and time-consuming nightmare for those who actually want to invest in the region. In certain respects, it is quicker and more efficient to undertake a new or "greenfield" investment in the region than to deal with procedures for valuing existing state-owned entities.

The former socialist economic planners of Eastern Europe demanded nothing of an enterprise except that it meet specific quantitative production goals during a certain plan period. A financial surplus at the end of the period was as likely to subject the enterprise manager to ridicule (he or she had obviously underordered inputs) as to praise. Losses were made up by direct government subsidies. Costs were determined by a labyrinthine network of contrived input prices and several artificial exchange rates. Energy imports from the USSR were accounted for at a fraction of the true world price. Contingent liabilities (and assets) inherited from the era of bureaucratic improvisation are vague. The distorted network of input and output prices used by socialist managers has been in large part destroyed since 1989. Yet a whole new set of problems in forecasting corporate performance during a time of unprecedented structural transformation and economic change has arisen. Ascertaining the true value of a potential asset or privatizable entity is an uncertain process, subject to political interference. Given the absence of viable domestic capital markets, it will be some time before the free market can be a neutral arbiter of corporate value.

Uncertainties and Irregularities in Privatization

Some uncertainty and confusion still exist among potential foreign investors about exactly what modes of acquisition are permissible and exactly how the privatization process in each of the countries of East Central Europe is to proceed. Most of this uncertainty is probably unnecessary. The inherently revolutionary nature of a privatization process taking place on an unprecedented economy-wide scale contributes to the perception that things are not completely under control. The proliferation of authorities with mandates for privatization at different levels (municipalities, republics, and federal agencies), the even greater proliferation of privatization programs and processes (such as mass, sectoral, spontaneous, trade purchases, liquidations), and lingering uncertainty over who actually has the greatest influence over approval of a potential deal (a government property agency, the local partner, or local politicians concerned with the deal's consequences for employment) all contribute to the opacity of the process. At the same time, such a diversity of programs and dispersion of influence may be the key to rapid if not entirely sufficient privatization.

Potential Western investors who initially enthused over Eastern Europe's prospects have become discouraged by irregularities or perceived corruption in all the countries concerned. The governments of Hungary, Poland, and Czechoslovakia have taken steps to centralize the privatization process in order to avoid charges of irregularity. At the same time they are trying to avoid the pitfalls of a privatization bureaucracy and the vestiges of central planning. Poland's daily revelations of corruption by the inherited communist *nomenklatura* and other members of the old boys' club eager to take advantage of the uncertainty and myriad market inefficiencies in the transition from socialism to capitalism make Poland the prime candidate for most corrupt transformation. All the East European countries are nonetheless rife with irregularity. It was made clear recently to a potential American investor by the state privatization agency of one of the most "Western" countries in the region that the Mercedes automobiles in the parking lot of a certain state-owned entity had been gifts to the managers from a competing Western supplier and that such practice was considered normal. Needless to say, the gift-givers are now the suppliers and the American company is pursuing investments in Asia. Although the solicitation of bribes may be expected of the communist remnants of Eastern Europe, it is no longer typical practice in Western European business.

Not All Countries Are Equal

As Hungary, Poland, and Czechoslovakia pursue the goals of a free-market economy and integration with Western Europe, it becomes increasingly difficult to generalize about the region. All three countries face the challenges delineated above, but Hungary is ahead of the others in finding solutions. This is reflected in the flow of foreign investment to the region. Hungary has only 10 percent of Eastern Europe's population, but was the recipient of more foreign private capital in 1991—over $1.4 billion worth—than all the other countries in the region combined. Relative political and economic stability, a dynamic private sector, international solvency, and a particularly pragmatic and flexible approach to privatization and direct foreign investment have helped lay the foundation for a significant contribution by international capital to the structural transformation of the Hungarian economy.

A particularly positive aspect in Hungary is the emergence of a viable private entrepreneurial sector making real contributions to the economy, significantly beyond the mere exploitation of market inefficiencies to make quick money. This self-generated private—not necessarily privatized—sector may be a promising destination for foreign direct and portfolio investment.[3]

Despite the common perception that the three countries of East Central Europe are the darlings of international investors, the fact that they remain generally insignificant on the level of global capital flows should be a small source of comfort to the countries of Southeastern Europe and the republics of the former Soviet Union. Although they are behind in the competition for international capital, their more glamorous competitors in East Central Europe are not necessarily far ahead.

There is no reason why the countries of Southeastern Europe could not thrive in competition by exploiting their own comparative advantages. Yugoslavia's civil war has unfortunately transformed one of the most promising economies in Eastern Europe into a basket case. Romania still faces a major political transformation. If Bulgaria's newly elected noncommunist government can instill some measure of confidence in its political system, a resolution is found to the country's daunting debt, and the economic stabilization program adopted in February 1991 is maintained, Bulgaria is best placed to fill a competitive niche. Relatively inexpensive yet skilled labor and a relatively liberal attitude toward foreign ownership could make Bulgaria as attractive to foreign investors as any of the East Central European states. Bulgaria's economy can be compared, at least potentially, with the thriving free-market economies of Turkey and Greece, rather than characterized by the chaos confronting its other Balkan neighbors.

Conclusion

The problems outlined in this chapter are not meant to cast fundamental doubts on the prospects for foreign involvement in the privatization process in East Central Europe. In fact, the region will likely be as attractive to private Western capital in the future as Southeast Asia and Latin America are currently. The initial excitement over the vast potential of the region during the collapse of communist regimes in 1989 was exaggerated, but so was the subsequent gloom when the daunting nature of the task ahead became clear. In fact, the real progress in transforming the centrally planned economies and the steady political will exhibited by all the new democratic governments in the region in the face of substantial opposition have been impressive. The process is unprecedented in world history, and thus the privatization plans must be ad hoc in nature. The recent Polish Foreign Investment Law and the official Hungarian stance toward restitution of property are examples of substantive actions to address the concerns of foreign investors. Considerably more flexible attitudes toward privatization and foreign involvement, in combination with real accomplishments in democratization, economic stabilization, and (to a lesser extent) structural reform, may well mean that East Central Europe's foreign investment potential can be realized and private capital flows may soon surpass the significant commitments of official public assistance.

Notes

[1]This author published *Discovering Investment Opportunities in Eastern Europe: A Framework* (New York: Salomon Brothers, Inc., July 1990), an initial survey of the potential attractions of the region to foreign investors, and is in the process of publishing an update of that appraisal.

[2]Per capita debt is scarcely a measure of capacity to pay. Sweden, Australia, New Zealand, and Canada have significantly higher per capita debts than Hungary, but their per capita incomes are also much higher. A more accurate measure, the ratio of debt to total convertible currency export income, reveals Hungary as heavily indebted, but places it in a better position than Poland, Bulgaria, Yugoslavia, or the former USSR. The Hungarian ratio also declined rapidly as exports to the West expanded during 1990–91.

[3]For a more extensive discussion of Hungary's accomplishments and challenges, see *Hungary: Reentering Europe* (New York: Salomon Brothers, Inc., April 1992).

Chapter 4

The Budapest Stock Exchange: Lessons and Challenges

József Rotyis

Act VI (on the public offering of securities and the stock exchange) took effect on February 1, 1990, creating the legal framework for a stock exchange in Hungary. On June 19, 1990, forty-one members founded the Budapest Stock Exchange (BSE), establishing it in accordance with the provisions of the law with an initial capital of 221,600,000 forints. At this founding general meeting, the members also passed the Charter of the Stock Exchange and elected senior officials. Also elected were the thirty arbitrators of the Arbitration Court of the Securities Market, which is authorized to settle disputes among issuers and traders.

The Budapest Stock Exchange trades two types of securities—listed and traded. (For a list of current securities, see Table 4.1.) The issuer of a listed security must meet certain minimum requirements: initial capital of 200 million forints, a minimum volume of stocks publicly issued or sold, and completion of at least one business year prior to listing on the BSE. Less rigorous capital and volume requirements are applied to traded securities. Licensed securities traders may sell or buy listed securities for their clients only on the stock exchange. Also, only listed securities can be traded on foreign official markets, and only after the required permits have been obtained from the National Bank of Hungary State Securities Supervision Board.

Trading on the BSE takes place every working day from 11:00 a.m. to 12:30 p.m., with open bidding from the floor. The licensed representatives of traders registered with the stock exchange make their offers and bids orally, and final prices are set

TABLE 4.1
SECURITIES TRADED ON BUDAPEST STOCK EXCHANGE

Listed	Traded
DUNAHOLDING RT.	AGRIMPEX RT.
FOTEX RT.	BONBON HEMINGWAY RT.
IBUSZ RT.	BUDA-FLAX RT.
KONZUM RT.	ELSÖ MAGYAR SZÖVETKEZETI
STYL RT.	SÖRGYÁR/MARTFÜ RT.
SZTRÁDA-SKÁLA RT.	KONTRAX IRODATECHNIKA RT.
ZALAKERÁMIA RT.	KONTRAX TELEKOM RT.
	MÜSZI RT.
	NITROIL RT.
	NOVOTRADE RT.
	SKÁLA-COOP RT.
	TERRAHOLDING RT.
	POSTABANK RT. (bond)

following an oral auction. Any trader may join the auction at any time. On September 18, 1991, a new trading method went into effect in conjunction with the open bidding system. An electronic public order book was implemented for two active stocks, a step which increased trading capacity.

On the trading floor, a small network of personal computers supports the dealing, with a display board providing information on transactions to brokers and visitors. Price and volume information is disseminated nationwide a few minutes after transactions occur through a national television network via a teletext system. A system operated by a private company also provides on-line information on transactions and offers to a smaller group of professionals. The vast majority of transactions are spot deals, but it is possible to enter into options and futures transactions. The settlement of these, however, is similar to that of spot transactions as no separate options and futures settlement system yet exists.

Transactions carried out on the BSE are cleared through the stock exchange by means of the central bank, the National Bank of Hungary. The stock exchange operates a central depository linked to the settlement system. For transactions carried out on the BSE, there is a rolling settlement system, and every transaction is settled on the fifth day following the date of transaction. The money and security positions of every broker are multilaterally netted out against those of all other members, which results in a determination of a single daily position for each broker in money and security respectively. A clearing fund is employed to minimize the risk to buyers and sellers of losses caused by the failure of a counterpart.

The state regulates the market of securities offered to the public through the State Securities Supervision Board, which was set up in accordance with Act VI. The role of the board is to issue the permits necessary to offer securities publicly, to license securities traders, and to supervise the market continuously. The board also supervises the operations of the BSE and approves the internal regulations of the exchange. Permission from the National Bank of Hungary is required to trade securities issued by Hungarian companies outside the country, as well as to issue and trade foreign securities in Hungary.

A self-regulated organization, the BSE also plays an important role in the regulation of the securities market. Its regulations govern trading, the settlement of transactions, and the securities listed on the BSE. Enforcement of these regulations is the responsibility of the stock exchange.

Following the establishment of the stock exchange, registered brokers founded the Association of Brokers, and, in 1991, securities trading companies formed the Association of Brokerage Firms in order to facilitate the work of the brokers and enhance cooperation among securities traders.

Economic Developments and the Securities Market in 1990–91

In 1990–91, economic conditions did not favor the development of the stock exchange and the expansion of securities trading. After the collapse of trade relations within the Council of Mutual Economic Assistance (CMEA) and the transformation of domestic economic structures, Hungary's gross domestic product (GDP) shrank 2.5 percent in 1990 after two years of stagnation, while prices to consumers increased at an annual rate of about 30 percent. Hungary's hard currency balance of payments in 1990, however, showed a surplus of $130 million. In light of the $1.4 billion deficit of 1989, this was a spectacular achievement. Hungary's foreign economic position continued to improve in 1991. Monetary restrictions and inflation have led to a general increase in average interest rates. This has meant that investment in debt securities is still uninviting, while purchasing shares has become more popular.

The 88-percent expansion during 1990 in the number of registered businesses operating as legal entities—an increase of 14,000 businesses—illustrates the progress of privatization. Most new enterprises, however, are small companies (primarily limited companies) run by a few people which, therefore, cannot raise capital immediately on the stock exchange. Twenty-eight percent of the new businesses were formed with the participation of foreign capital. International interest is demonstrated by the fact that the number of new companies established in 1991 is nearly three times higher than in the preceding few years, and the value of the overseas capital invested is approximately $1 billion.

As a result of accelerating inflation and rising interest rates, there were no signs of increased activity in the bond market in 1990, and there was only one bond issue with a par value of 100 million forints. The aggregate value of bonds held by private individuals has fallen, and the price of bonds has now reached 60–70 percent of par value. Short-term bond futures transactions offered by banks, however, have gained some popularity.

By the end of 1990, a total of 460 companies had been founded and registered as share companies, and fifty-six (or 12 percent) of them were issuing or selling shares publicly. The number of new public companies increased by eighteen in 1990, and fourteen companies publicly offered shares (with a total par value of 3.2 billion forints) for the first time during the first five months of 1991.

As in the 1980s, in 1990 the Hungarian government continued to issue debt securities, even though the new stock market did not follow suit. At the end of 1990, the volume of short-term, interest-bearing treasury bonds was 2.3 billion forints. These bonds were sold mainly to private individuals, and the higher volume represents a nominal increase of 35 percent. The sale of zero-coupon bonds issued to corporations and finance institutions increased by some 90 percent compared with the preceding year. The average market value of discount treasury bonds held at the end of each month was 8.1 billion forints in 1991. In December 1991, a new medium-term, floating-rate treasury bond series was issued at a nominal value of 15 billion forints.

Four companies largely privatized in 1990 and 1991 are now listed on the stock exchange. Privatization, however, has not really affected the stock exchange because shares from the twenty major companies sold under the First Privatization Program did not appear on the BSE until late 1991. In order to compensate the owners of property confiscated during the communist regime, the government has already begun issuing compensation bonds with an expected nominal value of 150 billion forints. The holder of a compensation bond is entitled to exchange it for privatized property.

The overall volume of trade on the BSE in 1990 was 7 billion forints, including both bond and share trading. Trading volume prior to the creation of the BSE was only 0.9 billion forints, approximately 12 percent of the total volume in 1990. During the six months following the establishment of the BSE, the average daily turnover was six times greater than during the six preceding months.[1] In the first eight months of 1991, the trading volume of the stock exchange was 6.6 billion forints. On the equity market, eighteen companies had their shares traded on the BSE with a total market capitalization of 45 billion forints in September 1991. Total trading volume (bonds, shares, and prompt, futures, and option transactions) in 1991 was 11 billion forints, the equivalent of $151 million.[2]

Cross-market comparisons of trading volumes show the potential of the Budapest exchange. The proportion of the average daily turnover in relation to the total market value of all shares (the turnover ratio) is similar to that of the Portuguese and Chilean markets. The BSE also compares favorably with regard to the average daily turnover per security. Some older, albeit smaller, stock exchanges have recorded lower levels of turnover in recent years than did the BSE in its first year of operation. For example, Vienna recorded a turnover volume of $114 million in 1984, Turkey reported $101 million in 1988, and the Venezuelan market, which produced outstanding results in 1990, traded only $93 million in 1989.

Trading volumes on the BSE have been boosted by the increase in the number of members, as well as the changing membership structure as the role of banks has decreased and that of the brokerage firms has increased. Although most trade is still conducted by a few members, the number of active participants also has increased.

While interest in investing in shares has risen markedly, bond trading has declined dramatically. In the first half of 1990, three-fourths of all trading was in bonds. In the second half of 1990, however, the proportion of bond trading to total market trading volume fell 13 percent, although the value of bonds traded actually increased slightly during that period. In December 1990, there was no bond trading at all, but bonds recently have been returning to the Budapest exchange. One bond was trading in September 1991, and a new treasury bond issue of 15 billion forints was expected to be introduced in December 1991.

In 1990 the average daily turnover was 17 million forints, with higher levels recorded only in the first few days following the founding of the BSE. In the first half of 1991, the average daily trading volume was 41 million forints, a 2.5–fold increase over the 1990 figure. Turnover volatility has increased. The value of futures and options transactions carried out between June 21, 1990, and May 31, 1991, was 1.4 billion forints, of which about 60 percent was initiated and concluded in 1990. Most of these transactions were options.

Most of the customers who permanently invest through the Budapest exchange are foreigners, both institutional and private investors. The dominance by foreign investors results from liberal laws governing foreign investment in Hungary, state guarantees of the repatriation of profits and capital gains, guaranteed convertibility for foreign investors, and an overall policy of permitting unrestricted foreign investment through the stock exchange. The number of domestic investors is still relatively small; about 25,000 Hungarians hold shares. Small savings, however, are likely to be concentrated in trading on the stock exchange only after the establishment of investment funds and institutional investors.

In 1990 the average market price/face value ratio,[3] reflecting the general change in prices on the BSE, rose quickly in July and then dropped in August. The price increase was followed by a drop in prices corresponding to world price decreases prompted by the crisis in the Persian Gulf. The price decline was temporarily slowed by several new flotations, but the prices of new shares decreased gradually in November and December 1990. In January 1991 prices remained low. A significant increase did not occur until March, when the prices of some securities rose 20–45 percent higher than their January levels. This increase was followed by another fall in May.

The Index of the Budapest Stock Exchange[4] gained more than 100 points during the first quarter of 1991. The total market value of shares officially introduced on the BSE between June 21, 1990, and September 18, 1991, also rose dramatically—the initial capitalization of 3.3 billion forints had increased to 45 billion forints by September 15, 1991.

The opening of the BSE in June 1990 coincided with the official listing of the shares of IBUSZ Rt., a bus manufacturer, with a par value of 480 million forints. This was then followed by five other securities introduced during the course of that year, and thirteen more in 1991.

Challenges and Solutions

The progress of the BSE shows that it is feasible to build a stock exchange even when a country's economy is in a deep recession and privatization proceeds more slowly than initially projected. Hungary has been successful because of its relatively strong private sector, the experience gained from twenty years of communist economic reform, and institutions that have emerged during the last decade. Now Hungary faces four more challenges. How they are met will shape the future of capital markets in that country.

Hungary's first challenge is *to increase the capacity and efficacy of the BSE, including its trading, settlement, and information systems.* The overall transformation of trading started in early 1990. At the beginning of 1992, the stock exchange began operating on a new floor much larger than the previous one and capable of handling higher trade volumes. Another priority is the continuous development of the settlement and depository systems. A settlement system and a depository serving the whole securities market will be established in 1992, giving new impetus to the development of the Hungarian securities market. Parallel to the improvement of the trading and settlement systems, the information system of the stock exchange will also be developed, which will broaden the range of current information on issuers and the market available to both the public and to professionals.

The second challenge is *to influence the balance on securities markets.* This includes, on one hand, the initiation of measures to stimulate and concentrate demand on the securities market (such as tax preferences for investors, favorable loan schemes for securities purchases, and definition of the legal framework for the operation of investment funds), and, on the other hand, enactment of measures to improve the quality of supply in order to make investments attractive even to smaller, more conservative investors.

The third challenge is, *given the importance of foreign investors in Hungarian capital markets, to link the Hungarian systems supporting the market to similar systems of national or international marketplaces.* There are two tasks about which foreign investors are most concerned: obtaining fast and reliable information on the market, and guaranteeing a settlement. Development of a system of information dissemination was scheduled for completion by September 1991. This system will link the floor of the exchange directly to major international information vendors, transmitting information both to and from the BSE. System links will be established both with national and international clearing and depository centers (in an arrangement similar to Euroclear and Cedel) to convey information about settlements.

The fourth challenge is *to build a capital market in an environment where a large number of potential and actual participants are unfamiliar with the nature and operations of the market.* For example, small domestic investors should be fully informed that investing in securities may result in loss, and professionals should be taught different techniques of limiting risk. A nationwide program is indispensable not only to development of the market, but also to increasing public confidence in it. The responsibility for designing and implementing such an educational program lies with the market institutions and, to a greater extent, with the government. A program of this type is not only in the interests of the market, but should also be considered a public service along the lines of health care education.

The four challenges articulated above can be addressed by the following measures:

- *Build a solid base for the central market first.* No stock exchange can survive over the long term without a large number of investors and professionals.
- *Avoid the physical allocation of securities.* This would lead to higher costs and could easily create a paperwork nightmare in the sparsely staffed offices of the market.
- *Stimulate domestic demand by tax preferences in order to encourage small investors.* Larger domestic liquidity will attract more foreign capital, which will result in greater overall market liquidity.

- *Start as simply as possible.* Investors and brokers need time to learn how the market operates. Full automation could reduce the transparency of the market.
- *Do not try to copy entire systems.* Pick the best parts of other systems and integrate in a way best suited to local conditions.
- *Seek flexible solutions in designing the legal framework of a capital market.* Relatively fast changes might be necessary if unexpected situations arise.

Notes

[1] Every trade figure in this report includes both sales and purchases.

[2] At the prevailing exchange rate on June 6, 1991, this figure is equivalent to $136 million.

[3] In calculating the ratio, the author considered officially floated securities only. The ratio is calculated as the simple arithmetic average of the monthly market-price/face-value ratio where each listed security has the same weight. In other words, different levels of market capitalization were not taken into account, and therefore the ratio does not truly reflect the movements of the market as a whole.

[4] The Council of the Budapest Stock Exchange decided in April 1991 that the stock exchange would publish, on an experimental basis, an index reflecting general market trends. The index reflects changes in the market value of the companies in the "basket" with a base of 1,000 as of January 2, 1991. The "index basket" includes the shares of certain companies whose liquidity and trading volume meet selected criteria. On May 31, 1991, the basket included six securities: Elsö Magyar Szövetkezeti Sörgyár/Martfü Rt., FOTEX Rt., IBUSZ Rt., MÜSZI Rt., SKÁLA-COOP Rt., and SZTRÁDA-SKÁLA Rt. The "index basket" is open. If other shares meet the requirements, the number of index securities may increase.

Chapter 5

Company Management and Capital Market Development in the Transition

Marvin R. Jackson

New institutions that would allocate and manage capital are badly needed in the transitional economies of Central and Eastern Europe. This chapter focuses on the connection between two lines of institutional development: the first, to promote private, nonpolitical ownership and control of enterprises responsible for the direct management of physical capital assets, and the second, to build up financial institutions that supply and manage credit or capital. The chapter begins with a brief review of financial institutions in the pre-1990 socialist economies and describes the progress of institutional change during the first two postrevolutionary years, 1990 and 1991. This background is useful in constructing an appraisal of alternative institutions in the West that might serve as models for Central and Eastern Europe. The chapter's final section explores what sort of capital market might be most useful in the period of transition from planned to market economies. The author argues that the issue is not which kind of capital market would serve best in a more fully developed market system, but which would best facilitate the most efficient and painless transition possible.

The Achilles' heel of socialism, according to Ludwig von Mises, is its inability to allocate capital rationally. The answers to his challenge coming from Oskar Lange and others—shadow prices for capital as well as goods—were never entirely satisfactory.[1] Furthermore, these economists' proposals for "market socialism" bore other weaknesses related to the establishment of effective product markets and managerial incentives. Two attempts to set up market socialism in Yugoslavia and Hungary, although faced with particular constraints, seemed to demonstrate all the weaknesses that von Mises warned against, in addition to the special problems of public choice associated with single-party states. Nevertheless, the great weakness of socialism, in either its orthodox central planning or its unorthodox market forms, was its inability to allocate capital effectively.

Pre-1989 Property Rights and Credit Problems in Eastern Europe

East European systems of property rights in 1989 already exhibited considerable diversity as a result of developments in the 1970s and 1980s, especially in Yugoslavia and Hungary. In the basic system, households had a more or less full set of rights over personal property, including houses and livestock but not land. Sometimes land was farmed in leasehold. Most other physical assets were limited to use or assignment rights attached to "offices" in the state administration. These included the rights of planners to set production targets, establish input-output norms, and allocate supplies, land, and capital equipment. The rights typically assigned to an enterprise manager were quite restricted, compared to those typical of a hired manager in the West. They came closer to resembling the prerogatives of shop foremen in the West. Income rights for managers and workers in production were distinguished by the general application of piece rates. In the managers' case, large shares of income came from complicated bonus arrangements, with major emphasis on fulfillment of the output plan, expressed in physical units or constant-price indicators. Many resources remained unassigned. When they were, the assignee had no particular incentive to preserve the value of the resource. For instance, the rivers under the control of a river administration charged with transportation or flood control simply became cheap public waste receptacles.

In conventional centrally planned economies, capital investments were allocated by central-planning methods which emphasized the growth of the productive capacity of priority sectors. Although physical input-output norms were used in the allocation process and sometimes imposed as plan targets for the users of capital, considerations of efficiency were generally ignored in favor of balanced growth.

The supply of money and credit was physically separated from the allocation of capital. Two distinct kinds of money were used: bank accounts for state enterprises and other institutions, and cash for transactions between the institutional and household sectors. Credit was initially used only as the temporary working capital of enterprises. Later, long-term credits for financing capital investments were used experimentally, as a way of encouraging enterprises to economize on the use of capital.

Privatization and Enterprise Management since 1989

Initial expectations that property in Central and Eastern Europe could be simply and swiftly privatized have been disappointed, despite the variety of methods used. These methods have included: (1) converting large state enterprises into joint-stock companies and selling their shares to both domestic and foreign private investors or their employees, (2) breaking up large state enterprises and selling or leasing the resulting smaller units, (3) selling or leasing small shops and service facilities, (4) reprivatizing or returning land, structures, and companies to previous private owners, and (5) allowing the formation of new small and medium-sized enterprises by individuals, private companies (sometimes with foreign participation), or authentic cooperatives. Following these various developments is not easy when different offices, even in the same country, sometimes release conflicting information on what has been or might be done. The need for more comprehensive and standardized statistical reporting is receiving attention in Hungary and Poland, where statistical bulletins now include lists of companies grouped by legal category.[2]

Nearly all approaches to privatization have encountered problems, although with hindsight most of these could have been expected in the process of bringing about a true institutional revolution. Shortages of trained personnel (such as lawyers, accountants, bankers, and entrepreneurs) have been a major obstacle, as have technical uncertainties over the new legal foundation for property rights and commercial codes. These problems have been compounded by legislative inexperience and inefficiency. Apparently simple schemes to create instant "people's capitalism" by issuing to all citizens vouchers or coupons which can be exchanged for ownership shares have not been followed by a single case of implementation, despite their political appeal. Conflicts have occurred over the spoils of ownership distribution and redistribution, a process approximating at times Marx's original "primitive accumulation of capital," fueled by substantiated and unsubstantiated fears of reduced employment, production, and income.

Where owner-managed enterprises are established or where privatization results in the same form of property, financial markets are still important for generating sources of investment capital, but they are of less value as a source of control over management. The main candidates for financial control are those enterprises whose managers are hired and do not personally own a controlling interest in the company they manage. This applies to three broad categories of enterprises: (1) state enterprises that are not to be privatized or that have not yet been privatized, (2) state enterprises that have been converted to joint-stock or limited-liability ownership, and (3) enterprises with predominantly foreign ownership. Since the latter is assumed to be controlled by forces in international markets and the country of origin of the investors, it is of no concern here.

The privatization attracting the most attention in every former socialist country is that of state enterprises. As is now well known, this process usually occurs in two stages: (1) conversion of a state enterprise into one or more joint-stock companies, and (2) the sale or distribution of the shares, which are originally (from the communist period as well) held by a state agency, to private persons or other companies, including banks. There are some exceptions, such as instances in which a decision is made to liquidate a state enterprise by selling its assets directly, in some cases to a workers' organization. Such conversions were first made possible by legislation enacted in Hungary, Poland, and Bulgaria in 1988, shortly before the political revolution. More recently, the approach to conversion in Hungary and Poland has centered on an investment bank or international accounting firm undertaking the conversion for a fee. The process of conversion includes decisions on which parts of the former state enterprise should be assembled into the new company and on what values of assets and liabilities (actives and passives) should appear on the company accounts. Asset evaluation is difficult because the old book values are economic nonsense. The new values should represent the present value of future net earnings, but who can guess what these are in the absence of markets, or even of reliable estimates of the future efficiency of the new companies? An alternative procedure might include demonopolization, breaking up enterprises into several separately managed units, or liquidation. In the case of liquidation, assets are often sold or leased to companies created by employees of the former state enterprise.

The controversial company-by-company privatization policies in Poland and Hungary were formulated in response to earlier denunciations of so-called *nomenklatura* privatization made possible under the 1988 conversion laws of Hungary, Poland, and Bulgaria. Charges that they were undervaluing assets also motivated officials to turn to Western experts. In order to establish a successful record from the beginning, the relevant agencies in Poland and Hungary began privatization with a small group of some of the soundest enterprises. Yet even in those cases, the process is proving more complex than anticipated, with public opinion shifting from criticism that privatization was conducted too fast to complaints that it is too slow.

In Hungary, the government's aim is to privatize 70 percent of all large state enterprises, but by late 1991 it had privatized only 8–10 percent, or about 330 companies out of 2,200 under consideration. Of those 2,200 state enterprises, 63 percent had been founded by ministries and 37 percent by local authorities. By 1990 their dominant form of control was self-management (as was the case also in Poland); only 32 percent of enterprises were state-administered, and 12 percent had been set up as wholly state-owned share companies.

Hungary's current program of privatizing large enterprises allows four methods: (1) "spontaneous privatization" initiated by the state-owned unit itself, (2) privatization initiated by the State Property Agency (SPA), (3) privatization initiated by domestic and foreign investors (a process which started in January 1991), and (4) privatization through the sale of component units of large state and local organizations for retailing, public catering, and services.

In September 1990, Hungary's SPA announced its carefully planned First Privatization Program, which covered twenty companies. Privatization was expected to be completed by mid-1991. Delays, however, ensued for technical as well as political reasons, and the sale of the first company's shares was rescheduled to begin in June 1992. The Second Privatization Program will cover some one hundred enterprises, including some state-owned ones that had been converted earlier into economic associations, plus several special cases: construction companies, historic vineyards, castles, and some existing monopolies.

Apart from the SPA-managed programs, it was expected that in 1991 another 200 spontaneous privatizations and 100 investor-initiated privatizations would take place. Thus, approximately 400 enterprises would cover about 20 percent of the book value of state assets. A program of similar magnitude was projected for 1992.

The ink had hardly dried on the final, "large" privatization program of Prime Minister Tadeusz Mazowiecki's government in late 1990, when it became clear that Poland would have a new government. Until then, most of the energy of its Ministry of Ownership Transformation (which is small when compared to Germany's Treuhandanstalt) had gone into a public stock offering of five companies. The new government of Prime Minister Jan Krzysztof Bielecki announced its program in February 1991. It maintained Mazowiecki's targets of reducing the state sector by half in three years and approximating a West European structure of ownership in five years. Later in 1991, however, the ministry revised these goals downward.[3]

Only one hundred to one hundred fifty of Poland's large enterprises, out of more than three thousand five hundred, had been privatized by all methods by the end of March 1991, a pace too slow for the Bielecki government. Two programs of "liquidation" have since been launched. The first, made possible by the State Enterprise Act, provided for the dissolution of 105 financially weak companies and the sale or scrapping of their assets. Under the second program, authorized by the Privatization Law of 1990, 138 enterprises were leased to their employees, or sold or turned over to commercial corporations. The Bielecki government also announced its readiness to push 400 of the biggest companies through a mass conversion in early 1991, so they could be purchased by the public with coupons and vouchers. The process was to be repeated for 300 more companies in early 1992, but both mass conversions remain undone.

In Czechoslovakia, the conversion of large-scale enterprises is barely underway. Privatization has been deferred until completion of a much-heralded coupon distribution, scheduled to begin in October 1991 and end in the second quarter of 1992. The distribution is now about five months behind this schedule.

Romania's government launched a massive program of conversion of state enterprises into joint-stock companies (in some cases, state companies) per legislation passed in late 1990. Another law, passed in August 1991, provides for privatization in which 30 percent of the shares will be distributed to adult citizens as "certificates of ownership" with a par value of 5,000 lei each which, after a certain time, will be marketable. The remaining 70 percent of shares will be managed by the State Ownership Fund for seven years, during which all shares must be sold off. There are also provisions for special sales to employees. Privatization of the first thirty companies was announced for 1992.[4]

Conversions and possible *nomenklatura* privatization followed from Bulgaria's conversion law of 1988 during the Todor Zhivkov and Andrei Lukanov regimes. Although a few statistics were published on forms of enterprise organization in early 1990, it appears that some early actions were either suspended or reversed. Bulgaria's program of privatization of large enterprises was relegislated amid great controversy. The first new series of privatizations, the auctioning of 80 agricultural and food-processing enterprises, was scheduled to start in September 1991.[5]

Recent Reforms of Banking and Financial Intermediaries

While little information is available on the privatization of property in Eastern Europe, even less is known about institutional changes in the banking system and among other financial intermediaries—especially investment funds, insurance companies, and pension funds. While it would be useful to analyze asset portfolios and the flow of funds, the scant information available permits only a general outline to be sketched.

In 1988 both Hungary and Bulgaria proposed a two-tier banking system in order to separate the functions of central banking from the functions of those banks providing enterprises and institutions with investment credits and receiving deposits from them and from the household sector. This banking system was implemented on a limited scale in Hungary, and ineffectively in Bulgaria. In 1989 a similar reform was initiated in Poland and the Soviet Union, and was extended to Czechoslovakia and Romania in 1990. The so-called commercial banks became the first financial intermediaries to be introduced in these countries since their postwar conversion to the Soviet system.

Czechoslovakia's two-tiered banking system was initiated on January 1, 1990, when the commercial activities of the Státni Banka were turned over to two new banks, Komercni Banka Praha and Vseobečna Uverová Banka Bratislava, plus the existing Investnicni Banka Praha. Under the current law, universal banks of the German type are permitted. New commercial banks, including private banks, were permitted as of January 1, 1991. By the end of that month there were twenty-six commercial banks with 26,280 employees and a 12.5 billion-crown capital. By January 31, 1991, there were also thirty-two representative offices of foreign banks (which were not engaged in commercial banking), five joint-venture banks with foreign participation, and three entirely foreign-owned banks established under the joint-venture legislation. By the third quarter of 1991, all banks were required to join a clearing system set up by the Státni Banka.[6]

Hungary's banking system was converted to two tiers in 1987, and in that year nineteen banking institutions were established, including five general commercial banks. By early 1991, the system included twelve commercial banks of mixed ownership, seven specialized financial institutions (some of which are scheduled to be converted into general commercial banks), the offshore Central European International Bank, and 260 savings cooperatives. Twenty-eight commercial banks and other banking institutions were members of the Hungarian Banking Association as of April 1991.

Hungary's 1991 banking law required banks to separate investment funds and stock-brokerage operations from commercial banking by January 1993. In response, the banks are setting up subsidiary operations. The Hungarian state still owns about 35 percent (33 billion forints' worth) of the banking system's capital. Foreign ownership amounts to about 13 percent, or 12.5 billion forints, of Hungary's bank capital.

A two-tiered banking system was established in Poland in January 1989, when nine state-owned commercial banks were founded by voivodships or provinces on the basis of local operations of the National Bank. By the end of 1990, sixty-three such banks were in operation, as well as 1,665 small cooperative banks, most of which had been subsidiaries of the Bank Gospodarki Żywnościowej (Food Sector Bank), made independent by law on January 20, 1990. In principle, Polish commercial banks can be universal banks, but this actually depends on each institution's charter.

A new state institution, Polski Bank Rozwoju SA (Development Bank of Poland), began operations in 1991 with the largest capital of any Polish bank. It was established specifically to lend to small and medium-sized enterprises, to restructure state enterprises, and to fund projects in energy conservation and environmental protection. It also distributes World Bank funds and establishes institutions, including mutual funds, for the development of capital markets.

By the end of 1990, Poland had twenty-four banks that could be considered private. This included twenty-two that were set up with 50 percent or more of private capital, and two originally established as state institutions that were privatized through the sale of stock. Private banks, however, remain relatively small. Their total balance-sheet capital does not yet equal that of any one of the regional state-owned banks created in 1989. One of the state-owned banks scheduled for privatization in 1991 was the Bank Rozwoju Eksportu SA (Export Development Bank).[7]

By the end of 1990, thirteen foreign-owned institutions, including six banks and seven representative offices, had been granted licenses to operate in Poland. The foreign banks had more capital than the private Polish banks, but less capital than the large state banks founded in 1989. Eight Polish banks also had minority (under 20 percent) foreign capital.

Stock Exchanges and Investment Funds

Hungary took the lead among East European countries by opening the Budapest Stock Exchange in June 1990. So far, trading on it has been limited to treasury paper, bank and enterprise bonds, and a slowly growing number of company stocks. Several investment funds based on both Hungarian and foreign funding also have been created, and they have already initiated limited direct investments.

The Budapest Stock Exchange listed fewer than ten stocks in early 1991. The total increased to nineteen by the end of the year, and was projected to rise to thirty to thirty-five by the end of 1992. Share performance has not been exciting since the rapid rise of IBUSZ Rt., a bus manufacturer, when the exchange opened. A share index computed from January 1991 declined from March through the last report. Open only ninety minutes each day, the exchange records a volume of transactions in shares only half of that recorded for Hungarian shares on the Vienna Exchange. Following a further definition of Hungarian banking law, the large Commercial Bank will set up facilities of its brokerage subsidiary, Pro Ltd., with eighty branches, which will make Pro Ltd. the country's largest brokerage operation. According to one Hungarian broker, a lack of institutional investors is the major weakness of the Budapest Stock Exchange. Probably none of the institutions concerned has been able to unhitch itself from the state budget, where most assets are invested in government bonds. Until pressure is taken off state budget revenues, share investments are likely to remain unimportant.

A stock market and investment funds were also launched later in 1990 in Poland, although their scale is much smaller than Hungary's, reflecting the more limited number of enterprises that so far have been converted into share companies. Unlike in Hungary, where banks are required to set up subsidiaries for stock market operations, the banks of Poland appear to be that country's most important brokers. Foreign-financed investment funds, including those from international agencies, have been established. In 1991, the Boston-based Pioneer Group filed the first application to Poland's Security Exchange Commission for permission to set up a fund aimed at ultimately investing up to $100 million from Polish investors.

Three Varieties of Western Capital Management

CAPITAL MANAGEMENT UNDER BUREAUCRATIC CONTROL

Adolph Berle and Gardner Means pointed to a weakness of the Western system of capital allocation resulting from what they called "the separation of ownership and property"[8]; others have since viewed this weakness as a "principal-agent problem." When professional managers run public companies whose shares are widely distributed among many relatively uninformed owners, the high transaction costs of organizing proxy collections mean that the average stockholder has no direct voice in the management of company assets and is left with no choice but to sell his shares if the dividends and capital gains are not satisfactory. Professional managers, many of whom come from their companies' ranks and own a few shares, appear to be free of share-owner control. If given the power of a monopoly in a weakly competitive market, managers acquire significant leverage to maximize their own wealth through their control over company assets. The problem can be compounded significantly through the organization of holding companies and through mergers, both horizontal and vertical. In these cases some planning by a responsible public office to compensate for market failure may be seen as a special need. One set of economists has perceived a need to counter the power of bureaucratic managers with the authority of public planners, while another has advocated "indicative planning" or "industrial policy" that could direct monopoly power toward the public interest and overcome market failures in the allocation of capital. Institutions to serve these goals exist in nearly all West European countries. None, however, seems to have attracted as much attention as Japan's Ministry for Industrial Trade and Industry, viewed by some as the key to Japanese growth and export success.

CAPITAL UNDER 'SOCIAL MANAGEMENT' AND 'EMPLOYEE OWNERSHIP'

One alternative or complement to oversight of enterprise management by state bureaucrats is to "socialize" enterprise management to increase the weight given to societal welfare and to reduce the tendency of managers to pursue their own financial advantage.

In the United States, for example, this was the goal of the school of "socially responsible management" that arose in the 1960s. In Europe, various national management models emerged under the influence of Christian Democratic movements.

A special form of "social management" was sought to enhance broader employee interest in capital management that increases the long-term returns to the employees. Aoki suggests that a key element in the large Japanese firm is "dual control by employees and financial interests."[9] The main fear raised by institutions seeking to increase employee involvement in management is that the workers will use their influence to increase their own share of net income to the detriment of efficient long-term investment. A similar fear is raised about the power of the bureaucratic managers. Employee control, however, in the right conditions, may raise long-term labor returns by increasing labor productivity and without misallocating capital.

CONTROL THROUGH CAPITAL MARKETS
AND FINANCIAL INSTITUTIONS

A third approach to the management of capital by nonowning, hired bureaucratic managers arises from the financial economies of American-style takeovers, and encompasses several institutional developments. Operating through financial intermediaries, this approach increases institutional ownership of equity shares and reduces individual ownership. In 1950, in both the United States and Britain, for example, individuals owned more than half the shares listed on major exchanges. By 1989, this proportion had fallen to about 21 percent in Britain and to a similar level in the United States. During this time, pension funds increased their proportion of shares from about 10 to over 30 percent, as did mutual funds and insurance companies. And, of course, outside the United States, the universal banks also held large portfolios of equities for their own investment accounts. Institutional ownership would be expected to improve supervision of capital use by reducing the ownership's transaction costs of monitoring and collecting proxies.

If a manager fails to earn the maximum return on his company's assets, the value of the company's shares on the stock market will be depressed. This reduces the manager's value on the labor market. In addition, it sets up the possibility that someone will purchase shares at depressed prices, gain control of the company, dismiss the manager, and, with better management, increase the value of assets and company shares. This would benefit not only the organizer of the takeover but also all other shareholders, some of whom would have sold their shares during the takeover bid.

Takeovers have been an especially important feature of capitalism since the late nineteenth century. In particular, the massive waves of mergers which marked the economies of the United States and Britain in the post-World War II period saw direct bids to the shareholders rather than merger negotiations between managements or boards of directors. Because this was often done in opposition to the existing corporate direction, the phenomenon has been described as a "hostile takeover." Hostile takeovers have also marked the restructuring and divesting of assets, which has tended to reverse some of the effects of the merger movement since the late 1980s. The dramatic effect of takeovers on the industrial organization of the United States and Great Britain has prompted an enormous amount of research to evaluate their effectiveness.

How do we evaluate the effectiveness of these takeovers? No convincing evidence has been collected to suggest that takeovers select only the efficient firms for survival or that they lead to a more profitable allocation of society's assets. That there is little difference between the firms taken and taking over may indicate that capital markets do, in fact, sufficiently discipline firms by the mere threat of takeover. But if this is so, why has there been so much takeover activity? Evidence from the merger movements of the 1960s and 1970s shows that larger firms tended to take over smaller ones with no subsequent increase in profitability. Thus, the result included neither increased efficiency nor exploited monopoly. It is possible that takeovers fulfilled the desire for more power or the need to remain competitive.

The rash of takeovers in the late 1980s involved in many cases the use of so-called junk bonds to finance leveraged buyouts by company managers. These involved spectacular gains, sometimes to persons violating the law and sometimes to managers who ruined companies that were already well-run or that had good long-range prospects. The fall in asset values and reduction in cash flow during 1989–90 led not only to the collapse of the junk bond market but also to sharp increases in defaults and compromise of the entire American financial system. Institutional investors in 1988 held the most junk bonds. Some 30 percent were held by insurance companies, 30 percent by mutual investment funds, 15 percent by pension funds, and 7 percent by thrift or savings and loan banks. Given government insurance on deposits, the banks could afford to gamble, while the others, despite their expert management, seriously underestimated the risk of default.

A definitive evaluation of American capital markets is yet to be made. Schleifer and Vishny recently published a model showing systematic bias in the pricing of short-term assets compared to long-term assets, which would suggest that leveraged buyouts and hostile takeovers can lead to the elimination of long-term investment projects.[10] Other empirical research suggests no evidence that buyouts are associated with lower expenditures on research and development, investments, or employment. Others show that the resulting increases in debt-to-equity ratios occur in stable industries such as food and tobacco, where higher ratios might be expected anyway.

A Choice of Models or of Policy Measures?

The American or institutional experience has tended to dominate the literature on financial economics, but it is not the only relevant model for the reform of financial institutions in Eastern Europe. In this region the more powerful example is the German model, or more broadly the Continental or Western European model, in which the German case may occupy one end of the spectrum and the British case the opposite end.

Formulating and using country models entails risks. The models can be oversimplified or inaccurately described. Moreover, significant changes are underway as a result of European unification, deregulation in the United States, and the application of regulations in Japan in response to the financial abuses which recently shook that country's markets and politics. In any case, there is no question of a country's financial institutions being adopted whole.

THE GERMAN MODEL

An alternative to the American system is the Continental system. Its most distinctly different case is that of Germany,[11] which features six significant characteristics:

1. Relatively few German companies have shares listed on the stock markets. According to figures cited by *The Economist* on April 27, 1991 (p. 46), slightly more than 600, or about one-quarter, of the AGs (*Aktiengesellschaften*, public limited companies) have listed shares. At the same time the total capital of all AGs is less than the combined capital of the private limited companies (GmbH, or *Gesellschaft mit beschränkter Haftung*).

2. Unlike in the American and British systems, where pension funds are invested widely, in Germany the common practice is to fund pensions with the shares of the employing companies. This significantly reduces the possibility of outside pressure, either through participation on company boards or external divestment of shares.

3. Outside takeovers are inhibited by the common practice of placing an upper limit on the holdings of any one shareholder.

4. Meeting all financing requirements depends largely on bank loans and much less on stocks or bonds. In 1970, 1980, and 1989, according to figures presented by *The Economist*, German nonfinancial companies used bank loans as the source of 90 percent or more of their net funds raised. (By contrast, the share of bank loans for French companies dropped over the same period from 80 to under 60 percent.)[12]

5. The universal banks play a major role in company governance. (The most important of these are the "big three," Deutsche Bank, Dresdner Bank, and Commerzbank, followed by a few large regional and cooperative banks.) The universal banks offer the full range of commercial and investment banking, plus brokerage services. The importance of these banks derives from their roles as a source of credit and as the underwriter of stock issues. Even though they are also subject to limits on their own holdings of shares, the universal banks acquire and vote the proxies of shares held for brokerage customers.

6. Company behavior can be monitored nearly continuously by loan officers. Questions have arisen about the effectiveness of doing this through members of the supervisory boards, given that they typically meet only twice a year. Furthermore, professional bankers generally are unlikely to intervene in the technical or marketing details of company management. It has been suggested, however, that the banks play a useful role in times of financial crisis, especially if companies must be restructured.

Even though Japan and Germany have laws with provisions similar to Chapter 11 of the U.S. Bankruptcy Act, they are seldom used. Instead, a private arrangement is made by the banks, which typically takes a long time to arrange. During this time, dividends and employment may be cut, but spending on investment and research and development is maintained. In contrast to the United States, where management often remains in place during the troubles, in Germany new management usually is brought in. The whole process reduces the likelihood of ultimate failure as well as creditors' potential losses.[13]

According to data from the *Monopolkommission* for the late 1970s, banks held 145 seats on the supervisory boards of the one hundred largest German industrial companies, or 9.8 percent of the total (far more than the banks' own shares in these companies). The banks were represented on sixty-one of the company boards of directors and supplied twenty chairmen and six deputy chairmen of the supervisory boards. Ninety-four of the 145 seats, or 64 percent, belonged to the three big banks.[14]

THE JAPANESE MODEL

In Japan, individual stockholders own only 30 percent of listed shares. Financial institutions, including insurance companies, own 40 percent. Japanese banks of all categories can invest in stock shares of nonfinancial companies, with a maximum holding of 5 percent of any one company's shares. For larger companies, a few important city banks will hold shares up to the limit and one of them will serve as the firm's main bank. This means that the bank maintains close ties to the company in cash management and credit operations. It will also manage loan consortiums. Until recently this was especially important because Japanese companies were financed with large ratios of debt to equity. This arrangement tends to insulate Japanese companies from outside takeovers. Also, although banks normally do not interfere in company management, if a company is in trouble the bank steps in and, if necessary, replaces the existing management, never with outsiders, but from among incumbent personnel. Companies associated with the most reputable banks almost never go bankrupt.

Aoki describes Japanese companies as subject to the dual control of internal managers and external bankers.[15] Although this might be considered detrimental to stockholders' interests, real rates of return to stockholders for the period 1963 to 1986 averaged nearly 12 percent. It would appear that stockholders and employees in long-term or lifetime jobs would share common interests.

Choosing Institutions for the Transition in Eastern Europe

Perhaps one-third of existing state enterprises in Eastern Europe produce goods of less total value than the cost of the energy and raw materials used to make them. Conversion of such state enterprises to joint-stock companies could resemble a massive bankruptcy process in which management may have to be changed, assets sold off or scrapped, debts reassessed, and both sides of the balance sheet reevaluated. Company governance is a major problem because there are few persons with the experience and training to serve on company boards. (In response to this problem, Poland has been running crash programs that offer some initial training.) A bigger problem is that most board members are appointed by state agencies and thus have no clear incentive to protect the value of assets.

Commercial banks generally are in poor financial condition and remain undercapitalized. For example, in 1991 Czechoslovak banks had capital-to-asset ratios of only 1 to 1.5 percent, far short of the Bank of International Settlement (BIS) requirement of 8 percent.[16] All banks have large portfolios of frozen bad assets. Institutional investors, insurance companies, and pension funds hold most of their assets in the form of government paper. How soon they will provide important stock investments is not known.

The reporting of information on both nonfinancial and financial companies is badly organized. Transactions take a long time to clear. As a consequence, even nascent financial markets are poorly organized. At this point, it might take longer to organize a broad, competitive system of specialized financial intermediaries than it would to strengthen the major banks and to tie them to the development of stock funds connected with voucher/coupon schemes. Thus, a German model (based on large universal banks) suggests itself as a useful institutional arrangement for the transition.

Notes

[1]Ludwig von Mises, *The Anti-Capitalist Mentality* (Princeton, N.J.: Van Nostrand, 1956); Oskar Lange and Fred Taylor, *On the Economic Theory of Socialism* (New York: A.M. Kelly, 1970).

[2]Kozponti, Statisztikai Hivatal, *Statisztikai havi közlemények*, vol. 4 (Budapest, 1991); Dept. Statystyki, *Biuletyn statystyczny* (Warsaw, 1991): 1–3.

[3]J. Lewandowski, "New Impulses for Privatization: Interview with Mr. Janusz Lewandowski, Minister of Ownership Changes," *Gazeta Przemyslowa*, as translated in *Economic Review* (Warsaw), May 21, 1991; Z. Fallenbuchl, "The New Government and Privatization," Radio Free Europe/Radio Liberty, *Report on Eastern Europe* (March 22, 1991): 11.

[4]M. Montias, "The Romanian Economy: A Survey of Current Problems," *European Economy,* special edition, no. 2 (1991): 177–98; M. R. Jackson, "The Progress on Privatization," Radio Free Europe/Radio Liberty, *Report on Eastern Europe,* vol. 2, no. 31 (August 2, 1991): 40.

[5]The data in this section are taken from a series of unpublished country papers presented at a conference on privatization in Eastern Europe, held in Ljubljana, Slovenia, November 7–8, 1990, and from Jackson, "The Progress on Privatization."

[6]Státni Banka Československa, *Czechoslovak Banking* (Prague: Author, 1991).

[7]P. Wyczanski and K. Nowinski, "A Study of Privatization in the Czech and Slovak Federal Republic," paper given at a conference on "Privatization in Eastern Europe," Ljubljana, Slovenia, November 7–8, 1991; M. Sowa, "System bankomy w Polsce," translated from *Rynki Zagraniczne,* no. 45, April 14, 1991.

[8]A. Berle and C. Gardener, *The Modern Corporation and Private Property* (New York: Harcourt, Brace, and World, 1968).

[9]M. Aoki, "Toward an Economic Model of the Japanese Firm," *Journal of Economic Literature,* vol. 28 (March 1990): 1–27.

[10]A. Schleifer and R. Vishny, "Equilibrium: Short Horizons of Investors and Firms," *American Economic Review,* vol. 80 (May 1990): 148–53.

[11]A. Hendrie, *Banking in the EEC: Structures and Sources of Finance* (London: Financial Times Business Information, 1988).

[12]"Survey of International Finance," *The Economist* (April 27, 1991): 46. A comparison of capital market financing in the single year 1987 by American and European nonfinancial corporations shows the stock (as opposed to the bond) share as 17 percent for the American companies and 67 percent for the European firms. This comparison probably reflects the special circumstances surrounding junk bond activity in the United States. Figures cited by Ingo Walter and Roy C. Smith, "European Investment Banking: Structure, Transaction Flow, and Regulations," in Jean Dermine, ed., *European Banking in the 1990s* (Oxford, England: Basil Blackwell, 1990), p. 108.

[13]"Survey of International Finance," *The Economist* (April 27, 1991): 25 and 49.

[14]John Cable, "Capital Market Information and Industrial Performance: The Role of the West German Banks," *The Economic Journal* (1985): 119–21.

[15]M. Aoki, "Toward an Economic Model of the Japanese Firm," *Journal of Economic Literature,* vol. 28 (March 1990): 1–27.

[16]M. Hrncir and J. Klacek, "Stabilization Policies and Currency Convertibility in Czechoslovakia," *European Economy,* special edition, no. 2 (1991): 17–39.

Chapter 6

Reforming Financial Systems in Eastern Europe: The Case of Bulgaria

Alfredo Thorne

Reform of the financial system is a key element in the overall economic transformation of the East European countries. In the short term such reform should contribute to stabilization by providing the authorities additional instruments for managing monetary policy and controlling inflation. In the medium term it should enhance the supply response by improving the allocation of resources. The reform process will be more difficult for the former East Bloc states than it has been for other developing countries. It is only a slight exaggeration to say that in Eastern Europe reforming the financial system will mean creating a new one from scratch. Most of the region's inherited financial systems are geared to the needs of a centrally planned economy, needs markedly different from those of a market economy.

This chapter represents an attempt to illustrate the type of problems that East European economies face in reforming their

The author is indebted to Zeljko Bogetic, Lawrence Brainard, William McCleary, Fabrizio Coricelli, Manuel Hinds, Colin Mayer, Roberto de Rezende Rocha, and John Wilton for very useful discussions and comments. The views expressed here are the author's own and do not represent those of the World Bank.

The author acknowledges possible flaws in Bulgarian financial data. For a discussion of the problems inherent with analyses of Bulgaria based on this information and methods that can be used to compensate, see Appendix 1.

financial systems, using the case of Bulgaria to illustrate the problems inherited by all of these economies and to make specific proposals for their solution. The author argues that Bulgaria, and other East European countries can indeed improve the supply response by reforming their financial systems. Such reform must: (1) link the financial sector reform to the privatization of enterprises and banks, (2) quickly privatize a group of banks, (3) encourage privatized banks to lend exclusively to the emerging private sector, and (4) turn the remaining banks into investment banks and make them participate in the process of restructuring and privatizing state-owned enterprises. This four-part strategy should stimulate the supply response by providing the emerging private sector more access to credit and by increasing savings deposited in the financial system.

The Current Financial System and Past Structural Issues

In this section the author presents an outline of the current financial system and the legacies of the communist economic structure. Those structural legacies are discussed in detail, with particular attention given to a remaining burden on Bulgarian bank portfolios: an immense if uncertain sum of nonperforming assets—that is, bad loans.

THE CURRENT FINANCIAL SYSTEM

By the end of 1990, the Bulgarian financial system consisted of the National Bank of Bulgaria (National Bank hereafter), the State Savings Bank (Savings Bank), and the Bulgarian Foreign Trade Bank (Foreign Trade Bank), plus eight specialized commercial banks, fifty-nine common commercial banks, and two private common commercial banks (the First Private Bank and the Agriculture and Credit Bank). All these banks had been established as shareholding companies and were licensed to operate as universal banks. Except for the two private banks, these banks were owned either by the National Bank, the Foreign Trade Bank, or public sector enterprises. Only eleven banks (including seven specialized commercial banks, the Foreign Trade Bank, and the Stroybank [a construction bank]) were authorized to open accounts and contract loans directly with foreign banks. Although common commercial banks could accept foreign-exchange deposits, they had to resell them to the Foreign Trade Bank for the lev equivalent.

Before 1981 the financial system consisted of the National Bank, the Foreign Trade Bank, and the Savings Bank. The National Bank, in addition to its duties as central bank, provided finance to and accepted deposits from the enterprise and government sectors. The Foreign Trade Bank specialized in foreign-exchange transactions. This role included contracting foreign loans with foreign banks on behalf of the government, accepting foreign-exchange deposits, and managing foreign-exchange reserves. The Foreign Trade Bank supplied loans to finance Bulgarian exports and provided prefinancing to importers and exporters. The Foreign Trade Bank was also responsible for administering foreign-exchange regulations, and was the authorized agent in relations with countries of the Council for Mutual Economic Assistance. The Savings Bank was created as a specialized institution to serve the household sector. It accepted household deposits, granted consumer and housing loans, and provided other bank services geared to households, such as management of the state lottery. The Savings Bank served as a net provider of funds to the system by depositing its excess funds with the National Bank.

Changes began in 1981, when the authorities created the Mineral Bank. The objective of this shareholding company was to provide finance to the enterprise sector for production above the targets set in the plan and for projects not included in the financial plan. In 1987, the National Bank established seven specialized banks and transferred most of its investment portfolio to them and the Mineral Bank, thus creating a two-tiered system of investment and commercial banks. These seven banks, plus the Mineral Bank, specialized in specific subsectors and in long-term investment finance. In May 1989, the National Bank adopted further changes, which took effect in early 1990. These entailed the creation of fifty-nine commercial banks out of the National Bank's former branches and the sale of the rest of the National Bank's branches to the commercial banks. Also, the two-tiered banking system was abolished, and all banks were allowed to function as universal banks. This enabled banks to provide short- and long-term loans, accept deposits from individuals and enterprises, and grant housing and consumer loans to individuals. All banks were transformed into shareholding companies, and the National Bank started selling its bank shares to public-sector enterprises.

The changes leading to the creation of both specialized banks and common banks implied that there would be a major transfer of resources from the National Bank to the commercial banks. In 1987, the National Bank created the specialized commercial banks by transferring the equivalent of 33 percent of Bulgaria's gross domestic product (GDP) in enterprise-sector assets and by granting loans equivalent to 36 percent of GDP. As a result, the National Bank's enterprise sector assets fell from 89 percent of GDP in 1986 to 51 percent in 1987. Similarly, in 1990, the National Bank created the fifty-nine common commercial banks by transferring 40 percent of GDP in enterprise-sector assets and 22 percent of GDP in demand deposits, and by granting loans equivalent to 20 percent of GDP. As a result, the National Bank's enterprise-sector assets fell from 51 percent of GDP in December 1989 to nothing in March 1990, and demand deposits dropped from 26 percent of GDP in December 1989 to nothing in March 1990. The specialized and common commercial banks were created, however, with no additional infusion of capital.

The creation of the specialized and common commercial banks and the conversion to universal banking allowed greater competition among banks, but in fact little else was changed. Specialized commercial banks began to diversify their lending into sectors other than the ones for which they were established and into short-term lending, while common commercial banks started attracting more deposits and diversifying their lending. In an attempt to diversify the common commercial banks' and specialized commercial banks' ownership, the National Bank sold these banks' shares to public-sector enterprises. But in spite of government efforts to broaden the structure of the financial system and to enhance competition and bank response, the financial system still changed very little.

Following is a brief description of the nine most salient structural problems the financial system was experiencing at the end of 1990, that is, before the new noncommunist authorities launched their reform of the financial system.[1]

Segmentation.   The financial system was split into segments in terms of both size (deposits, capital, and assets) and area of specialization (Table 6.1). The pre-1987 segmentation still pre-

Table 6.1
Liabilities and Assets by Groups of Banks, 1990, as Percentage of Total

	Sources of Funds				Assets			
	Deposits^a	Central Govt's Credits	NBB's Credits^b	Credits Foreign Exchange^c	Capital^d	Other Net^e	Total	Net of Clearing^f
NBB*	15.8%	0.0%	0.0%	0.0%	56.5%	12.0%	23.7%	20.5%
SSB*	46.2%	1.5%	0.0%	0.1%	2.8%	4.0%	13.3%	13.9%
BFTB*	10.1%	3.1%	1.2%	93.6%	13.1%	64.7%	23.5%	24.4%
SCB*	11.2%	1.0%	60.8%	6.3%	16.1%	32.0%	15.1%	15.7%
CCB*	16.8%	94.5%	38.0%	0.0%	11.4%	−12.7%	24.5%	25.5%
Of the CCBs^g:								
Largest five	44.4%	n.a.	3.18%	n.a.	24.6%	n.a.	56.3%	
Smallest five	1.0%	n.a.	0.6%	n.a.	3.4%	n.a.	0.7%	

Source: National Bank of Bulgaria, Monetary Survey.

* NBB (National Bank of Bulgaria), SSB (State Savings Bank), BFTB (Bulgarian Foreign Trade Bank), SCB (Specialized Commercial Banks), CCB (Common Commercial Banks)

Notes: (a) In the case of the National Bank, this consists of currency outside banks, plus time, savings, and foreign currency deposits, and for the other banks consists of demand deposits; time, savings, and foreign currency deposits; and import and restricted deposits. Total common commercial banks' deposits exclude municipalities' demand deposits in line with the IMF's methodological guidelines for 1990 Monetary Survey estimates. (b) Consists of the National Bank's loans to banks recorded in the Monetary Survey as "Credit from National Bank" and "Other Liabilities"; excludes the National Bank's loans for the purpose of the clearing system. (c) Excludes foreign currency deposits. (d) Defined as the paid-in capital and excludes noncapitalized retained profits and reserves. (e) Defined as the Monetary Survey's item "Other Items, Net," and excludes the National Bank's loans to common commercial banks and specialized commercial banks and the valuation effect of foreign-exchange loans granted, in the case of the Foreign Trade Bank. Both of these are classified in "Other Items, Net" in the Monetary Survey. The valuation effect is recorded in "Other Accounts Receivable." (f) Excludes "Other Assets," which consist mainly of the outstanding amounts in the clearing system. (g) Indicates the proportion concentrated by the largest (or smallest) five of the fifty-nine Common Commercial Banks. Largest (and smallest) five banks are defined in relation to each variable, for example, deposits, capital, assets.

vailed, despite diversification measures. The National Bank was the largest bank, accounting for 23 percent of total assets and for 57 percent of total capital; the Savings Bank specialized in the housing sector and accounted for 46 percent of the deposits; and the Foreign Trade Bank specialized in foreign-exchange transactions and accounted for 93 percent of total foreign-exchange liabilities. In contrast, specialized commercial banks and common commercial banks accounted for a very small share of banking business. Fully owned and controlled by the National Bank, they lacked independence. Moreover, while the Savings Bank accounted for most of the deposits, predominantly from households, only a portion was used to finance mortgages. The National Bank used the Savings Bank deposits to fund the specialized commercial banks and common commercial banks.

Concentration.   At the end of 1990, the three largest banks held most of the assets, deposits, and capital while the sixty-seven commercial banks held only a very small share. In fact, the Bulgarian financial system was characterized by the coexistence of very large banks with very small banks. Respectively, the National Bank, the Savings Bank, and the Foreign Trade Bank (see Table 6.1) held 24 percent, 13 percent, and 23 percent of total assets; 16 percent, 46 percent, and 10 percent of total deposits; and 56 percent, 3 percent, and 13 percent of total capital. By contrast and on average, each specialized commercial bank accounted for 1.8 percent of total assets, 1.4 percent of total deposits, and 2.0 percent of total capital; each common commercial bank accounted for 0.4 percent of total assets, 0.6 percent of total deposits, and 0.2 percent of total capital. Concentration has also been a problem within the common commercial banks. The largest five banks, in terms of deposits, held 44 percent of total common commercial banks' deposits, and the smallest five held only 1 percent of total common commercial banks' deposits. The situation is similar for assets and capital. The largest five common commercial banks, in terms of assets and capital, held 56 and 25 percent of the common commercial banks' total assets and capital, while the smallest five held 0.6 and 3.4 percent, respectively.[2]

Reliance on National Bank credits.   A key feature of the Bulgarian financial system at the end of 1990 was the specialized commercial banks' and common commercial banks' reliance on National Bank credit. The result was an odd situation in which the National Bank had to borrow the Savings Banks' excess deposits to provide specialized commercial banks and common commercial banks with the necessary funds for their lending. As is explained in more detail later in this chapter, interest rates had very little to do with this distortion, which resulted from the way in which the National Bank established these banks—by transferring both its loan portfolio and the necessary finance. This kind of dependence indicates that banks had accomplished little in terms of diversifying their sources of funds. (See Table 6.1). The eight specialized commercial banks held 61 percent of total National Bank credits, and the fifty-nine common commercial banks held 38 percent. This reliance can be measured more accurately by using the ratio of total National Bank credit to total commercial bank assets. On average, the specialized commercial banks' ratio was 57 percent and the common commercial banks' was 22 percent. Of the eight specialized commercial banks, six had a ratio greater than 30 percent, and of the fifty-nine common commercial banks, twenty-three had a ratio greater than 30 percent. Moreover, most of the National Bank's credit to common commercial banks was held by only a few of these banks. For instance, 32 percent of National Bank credit to common commercial banks was held by the five largest common banks (in terms of National Bank credits), and 0.6 percent by the five smallest common commercial banks.

Branch concentration.   The number of bank branches per inhabitant as of late 1990 was low when compared to branch distribution in countries with the same level of development. More important, these few bank branches were owned by one bank, the Savings Bank. This branch concentration in turn contributed to the Savings Bank's deposit concentration and to commercial bank reliance on the National Bank's credits. The Savings Bank owned 3,915 places of business out of the financial system's total of 4,129, and 242 branches out of a total of 356. By contrast, each specialized commercial bank owned on average six places of business and no branches, and each common commercial bank owned three places of business and two branches. Contributing to this imbalance was the design of the post-1987 changes. Both the specialized and common commercial banks were created as banks without branches. Since then, the lack of dynamic, independent bank management and the absence of a real-estate market have discouraged banks from increasing the number of branches.

Insufficient capital.   Bulgarian banks' capital at the end of 1990 was small relative to their volume of assets, and, more important, to their volume of nonperforming assets. Banks had on average a ratio of capital-to-risk assets of 5 percent, well below the 8 percent recommended by the Basel agreement. This average ratio, however, understated the extent to which banks were undercapitalized. While the Basel agreement defines assets to exclude nonperforming assets, in Bulgaria asset definition included them. As is discussed later in this chapter, Bulgarian banks held a large proportion of nonperforming assets. The ratio of capital-to-risk assets varied among banks. In general, excluding the National Bank, the largest banks in terms of assets had the lowest capital-to-risk ratio. The two largest banks, the Savings Bank and the Foreign Trade Bank, had ratios of 1 and 3 percent, respectively. Although specialized and common commercial banks had on average ratios of 5 and 2 percent, respectively, five of the eight specialized commercial banks—which accounted for 80 percent of specialized commercial banks' assets—had ratios below 5 percent, and the five largest common commercial banks, in terms of assets, had ratios of less than 1 percent.

Profitability.   Banks' reported profits, although very high by international standards, failed to measure profitability accurately for two reasons. First, recorded profits were accrued totals and thus included interest income that had not actually been paid. Second, banks were not forced to make provisions for loans in arrears and in moratorium. Had banks been pushed to make provisions for these loans, their profits would have been smaller. Bulgarian banks held these loans without being forced to make provisions, despite the fact that by the end of 1990 regulation on bank provisioning had been in place for three years. Until 1991, banks were not forced to comply with such regulations or to classify their loans on the basis of performance.

Ownership.   Bank ownership in Bulgaria in late 1990 was characterized by a conflict of interest. The National Bank was the major shareholder of the specialized and common commercial banks. Other important shareholders were the Foreign Trade

Bank and public-sector enterprises. National Bank ownership of banks posed a conflict of interest because the National Bank was the owner of these banks, as well as the institution responsible for supervising and controlling them. To remove this conflict, the National Bank started selling its shares in specialized and common commercial banks in 1990. Major buyers, however, turned out to be public-sector enterprises and other banks; these enterprises were also major borrowers from these banks. In many cases, borrowers with problem loans bought banks' shares to guarantee continuous access to credit. Banks bought each other's shares to reduce their dependence on the National Bank. This ownership of banks by public-sector enterprises can limit the banks' ability to collect loans by exerting pressure on public-sector borrowers. (In other socialist countries, such as Yugoslavia, this has been a major factor explaining large losses by banks.[3]) Loss of bank control by the National Bank, as a result of the sale of shares to public-sector enterprises and banks, opens up the possibility of "spontaneous" privatization. Although in principle there is nothing wrong with bank privatization, it is not desirable to sell troubled banks to the private sector because the result can be bank failures and a loss of private sector confidence in privatization.

Payments system.   In Bulgaria, banks' checking accounts were underdeveloped and the procedure for clearing outstanding accounts took a very long time to develop.[4] Both these problems led to the use of cash by individuals and enterprises as the primary means of payment and to the accumulation of large, outstanding, unsettled balances between banks. The persistence of large outstanding balances in banks resulted in an excessively large stock of base money, which was rationalized as being a result of the inefficiency of the payment system. Large outstanding balances can create inflationary pressures if they turn into currency. The National Bank started improving the payment system by creating Bankservice, a fully owned subsidiary in charge of the clearing system, but progress had been insufficient as of late 1990.

Management.   Bulgaria's bank managers lack the necessary skills to manage banks in a market economy. Most bankers had been trained to manage a bank in a system where the concept of risk and return on assets and liabilities was absent. Bankers were responsible only for executing orders from the National Bank. The transition to a market economy, however, requires bankers capable of assessing risk and borrowers able to repay loans. This requires retraining incumbent bankers, developing the banking profession, or both. As of late 1990, the Savings Bank and Foreign Trade Bank bankers appeared to have the potential to become professional bankers if some training were provided.

In addition to suffering from structural problems, the former Bulgarian banking system had also helped sustain unprofitable enterprises in the way that it financed the public sector. Government authorities controlled credit allocation through a system of credit targets and limits on the quantity of credit. This control, however, failed to prevent inefficiencies and did not facilitate financial restraint because authorities frequently overruled their own credit targets in order to finance the government's five-year plans. A very high involuntary demand for money further expanded the supply of credit. This strong demand is revealed by a high M2-to-GDP ratio (M2 being currency plus all bank deposits).

The high demand for money combined with a lagging supply of goods produced a "monetary overhang" and the threat of inflation. The two most important causes on the supply side were the shortfalls of available goods and the small number of financial assets offered by the financial system. This disequilibrium in the goods market was in turn caused by the authorities' policy of guaranteeing a stable income to wage earners by controlling prices, the nominal exchange rate, the nominal interest rate, and nominal wages, regardless of productivity.

Success in dealing with monetary overhang requires authorities to take steps to limit the effect of excess money stock on inflation. Unfortunately, some inflation seems unavoidable. International experience with monetary overhang indicates that even countries that opt for monetary reform experience high inflation if they failed to adopt anti-inflationary policies when an excess money supply began to ignite price increases.

NONPERFORMING ASSETS AND THEIR EFFECTS

The true extent of nonperforming assets in bank portfolios is uncertain, although they are believed to be sizeable relative to total loans. Two factors make quantification difficult. The first is relative price distortion. Monetary authorities can quantify bad bank loans only when they know the effect of the change in relative prices on an enterprise's financial situation. Such a relative price change would result from introducing market forces and lifting price controls. (It is possible that some loans to enterprises which appeared to be productive became nonperforming when relative prices changed, and vice versa.) The second factor is the deficiency in bank and enterprise accounting plans. Bank and enterprise balance sheets audited by international auditors are unavailable. Also, as explained above, the differences between Bulgarian and Western accounting plans can lead to difficulties in loan classification. As noted earlier, banks were not compelled to classify their loans according to performance, to make provisions on troubled loans, or to adjust their capital according to risk under the communist regime.

Estimating the size of banks' unproductive assets is important because it enables the authorities to quantify the cost of restructuring the financial system. This can have an important effect on the design of strategies to reform and privatize the financial system. In particular, it is important to know how large the banks' current losses are (what their cash-flow shortfall is) and what proportion of their total assets are nonperforming or to learn the value of their net worth adjusted for unproductive assets. Answering the first question provides an estimate of the cost to the government of keeping these troubled banks operating, and answering the second indicates the cost (in net present value) of a bank cleanup. (The fiscal cost of the cleanup, however, will vary depending on the type of scheme adopted and the number of years over which cost is spread.)

There are two sources of nonperforming assets, both of them related to bank loans to public-sector enterprises. The first source is the public enterprise loans, denominated in leva, which were transferred by the National Bank to both types of commercial banks. The second source is the foreign-exchange risk assumed by the banks when they lent to enterprises. As explained above, the Foreign Trade Bank granted lev-denominated loans to enterprises and financed these loans by borrowing in convertible currencies. Although more nonperforming loans may have been made by specialized commercial banks after 1987 and common commercial banks in 1990, they are believed to be relatively small in number. Moreover, although the government (through the Financing Plan) compelled banks to grant these loans to enterprises, they are considered a public-sector liability.

Despite the reasons already provided, it is hard to offer an accurate estimate of the extent of lev-denominated, unproductive loans. Anecdotal information suggests that a crude estimate can be made by assuming that these loans were equivalent to the deposits transferred by the National Bank to the specialized and common commercial banks when they were established (see Table 6.2).[5] In fact, since 1987 the National Bank has been unable to recover these deposits from the commercial banks. This became particularly evident in early 1991 when the interbank market was established and the National Bank had to give special treatment to these deposits.[6] This estimate of nonperforming loans assumes that 54 percent of the enterprises' loans transferred by the National Bank to specialized and common commercial banks became nonproductive. In terms of their distribution between specialized and common commercial banks, about two-thirds went to the specialized commercial banks and one-third to the common commercial banks. These represent two-thirds of all the specialized commercial banks' extended loans and two-fifths of such loans by common commercial banks.

TABLE 6.2

ESTIMATES OF EXTENT OF NONPERFORMING BANK LOANS
(END OF 1990)

	Total for commercial banks	Specialized commercial banks	Common commercial banks
In billions of leva	21.3	13.3	8.0
As share of GDP	34.4%	21.4%	12.9%
As share of banks' extended loans	53.9%	64.6%	42.3%

SOURCE: National Bank of Bulgaria, Monetary Survey.

The effect of the troubled loans on individual banks' balance sheets is limited because the National Bank's deposits are equivalent to the amount of nonperforming loans, and their distribution among banks is similar to that of the nonperforming loans. This is because the National Bank established specialized commercial banks and common commercial banks by transferring the same proportion of loans and deposits. Unproductive loans, however, have had an impact on the National Bank's net worth and cash flow because the National Bank funded specialized and common commercial banks' deposits by borrowing from the Savings Bank (through higher reserve requirements). While the National Bank has to pay interest on Savings Bank loans, it might not receive payment on the interest on the commercial bank deposits. This results in a deficit for the central bank. This is worrisome because it could make monetary policy endogenous; the National Bank can finance this cash-flow deficit only through monetary expansion.[7] This could happen if enterprises fail to service their commercial banks debts, and the banks decide to finance this shortfall by running arrears on National Bank deposits. In that case, the National Bank will have to finance its interest shortfall by expanding monetary reserves.

The second source of nonperforming assets is bank-assumed foreign-exchange risk (the Foreign Trade Bank's foreign-exchange losses). Bank foreign-exchange risk is defined as the sum of total net foreign-exchange liabilities and total foreign-exchange deposits minus enterprises' foreign-exchange credits.[8] Defined in this way, bank foreign-exchange risk indicates the cost to banks of assuming enterprises' foreign-exchange risk. Estimates indicate that most of this risk was assumed by the Foreign Trade Bank, and thus the main effect has been on its net worth and cash flow. In general, the greater the foreign-exchange risk, the lower the net worth and the greater the cash-flow shortfall. Foreign-exchange risk equaled about 8 percent of GDP in 1986 and 39 percent in 1990 (see Table 6.3). Measured as the ratio of total Foreign Trade Bank assets, it was 23 percent in 1986 and 54 percent in 1990.

The 1989 hike in the inflation rate and the devaluation of the lev against international currencies in 1990 also affected lev-denominated nonperforming assets and foreign-exchange risk.

TABLE 6.3

ESTIMATE OF BANKS' ASSUMED FOREIGN-EXCHANGE RISK

(PERCENTAGE OF GDP)

	1986	1990
Total Banks	8.0	38.9
Of which: Foreign Trade Bank	8.0	38.5

SOURCE: National Bank of Bulgaria, Monetary Survey.

The fall in real interest rates as a result of the increase in the inflation rate decreased the *real* value of commercial banks' lev-denominated, nonperforming assets, of National Bank deposits, and of Savings Bank reserve requirements—thus the effect of these assets on National Bank cash flow. By contrast, the 1990 devaluation of the lev increased the *real lev* value of the Foreign Trade Bank's foreign-exchange risk and reduced the bank's profitability. This effect on the Foreign Trade Bank (and thus on the budget) has gone unnoticed because of the government moratorium on the Foreign Trade Bank's foreign creditors. Its effect will depend on the conclusion of the foreign debt negotiations currently underway between the Bulgarian authorities and their foreign creditors.

Bulgarian Financial Reform in 1991

In February 1991, the Bulgarian government started adopting measures to correct problems in the financial sector. These steps were part of an economic reform program aimed at transforming the Bulgarian economy into a market economy, a program supported both by an International Monetary Fund standby loan and a World Bank structural adjustment loan. Among the most important measures concerning the financial sector were the monetary and credit measures designed to correct credit allocation and monetary overhang, and the institutional reform measures devised in coordination with the World Bank in July 1991.

MONETARY AND CREDIT POLICY

In February 1991, the Bulgarian government began to use monetary and credit measures to reduce the monetary overhang of a money supply already high relative to GDP and to restrain further inflationary pressures caused by new currency emissions. The authorities combined these monetary and credit measures with a wage policy, hoping to use wage restraint as a nominal anchor to control inflationary expectations during the first half of 1991. The government negotiated nominal wage increases with trade unions and employees for the first and second quarters of 1991.

Preliminary results indicated that the monetary and credit measures, in concert with other stabilization measures, were

successful in reducing monetary overhang and controlling inflation. The monetary overhang, measured as the ratio of M2 to
GDP (M2 being currency plus all bank deposits), fell from 83
percent at the end of 1990 to 47 percent by June 1991.[9] This
decrease in overhang also cut back the *real* stock of credit denominated in leva; however, it increased the banks' foreign-exchange
losses. The reduction in lev-denominated credits resulted from
the high inflation of the first quarter of 1991, while the increase
in the foreign-exchange losses resulted from the nominal devaluation of the lev. The inflation rate and the exchange rate were
stabilized by a combination of monetary, credit, and exchange-
rate policies. After reaching an annual rate of 111 percent in
February, the rate of inflation fell to 56 percent in March, 3.5
percent in April, and 2.5 percent in June 1991. In some respects,
the monetary and credit measures were more successful than
other stabilization programs that used the exchange rate as a
nominal anchor (as was done in Poland) because it stabilized
inflationary expectations without having to fix the nominal exchange rate. This approach avoided overvaluation of the real exchange rate and a resulting pressure to reduce exports.

Bulgarian authorities reduced the monetary overhang and
controlled inflationary pressure by lifting price controls on most
goods while making monetary holdings more attractive. Monetary holdings were made more attractive by:

1. *Increasing interest rates.* The government increased the basic
    interest rate (BIR)—the rate at which the National Bank lends
    to other banks—from 4.5 percent in December 1990 to 15
    percent in January 1991, 45 percent in February 1991, and 52
    percent in June 1991. The government intends to continue
    adjusting the BIR periodically in line with domestic prices
    and the exchange rate. It has also lifted interest-rate restric-
    tions on banks and expects them to fix their interest on de-
    posits and loans in response to market conditions (excess
    demand for funds) and to changes in the BIR.[10] Although
    interest rates on certain types of preferential credit, such as
    housing loans, were also increased, they were fixed below
    market levels.

2. *Issuing government securities.* The government began to issue
    bonds and treasury bills to induce asset holders to reduce
    their monetary holdings. It issued one-year treasury bonds
    in December 1990 and treasury bills in early 1991. The bonds

yielded an effective annual interest rate of 43.7 percent, and the treasury bills an effective annual rate of 31.1 percent.

3. *Stimulating prepayment of consumer and mortgage loans.* The government allowed consumer and mortgage borrowers to repay their loans at pre-February 1991 interest rates.

As another way of controlling inflationary pressures, the Bulgarian government imposed tight credit limits and increased reserve requirements. Credit limits provided for a maximum *nominal credit expansion* of 15 percent between the end of December 1990 and the end of June 1991 and for a government *nominal credit contraction* of 16 percent between December 1990 and June 1991.[11] The government reduced credit expansion further by increasing reserve requirements on bank liabilities from 5 percent at the end of 1990 to 7 percent in February 1991. These tight credit policies were reinforced by the policy of high interest rates, which monetary authorities expect will reduce demand for credit.

Once inflationary expectations subside, the government expects to shift from direct to indirect monetary control by developing the domestic and foreign currency interbank markets and the market for government bonds and treasury bills. In February 1991, Bulgarian authorities liberalized the exchange-rate market, and banks were allowed to base their buying and selling rates on market conditions.[12] The authorities have also established an interbank market for domestic currency. The Savings Bank is no longer required to place its excess deposits with the National Bank,[13] and banks are allowed to borrow and lend from each other on terms they decide. The National Bank has limited its credit to other banks to 20 percent of their needs. (This, however, excludes National Bank credit used by banks to finance loans in difficulties.)

Despite initial success, some serious allocation problems have arisen. First, the government credit ceiling was exceeded because of the government's difficulty in reducing its deficit and because of expanding credit to the government.[14] Second, banks have allowed enterprises to capitalize their interest on loans. This has been the result of the sharp increase in interest cost and the severe recession. As a result, credit has been held back from the sectors that should receive more credit, while the sectors that should be adjusting (government and public-sector enterprises) have benefited from the credit expansion.

PLANS FOR INSTITUTIONAL RESTRUCTURING

To address the financial system's structural problems, the government agreed in 1991 with the World Bank on a two-phase program. In the first phase the government promised to: (1) establish a Bank Consolidation Company (BCC); (2) organize bank mergers; (3) establish a legal and regulatory framework; and (4) restructure banks' bad-loan portfolios. In the second phase, the government promised to undertake a financial-sector reform based on a fresh study of the financial system.

Bank Consolidation Company.   The government will establish the BCC as a way of assuring direct control of state-owned banks. This measure is aimed at ending the interlocking relationships between banks and their clients, which are mostly public-sector enterprises (PSEs). Every PSE owning bank shares would exchange its shares for BCC shares. This applies only to banks established as joint-stock companies, thus excluding the Savings Bank. The BCC's principal responsibility will be to undertake bank mergers.

Bank mergers.   The BCC pledged to merge the large number of small banks into some ten medium-sized, economically viable banks. Initially, the BCC will concentrate on institutions unable to comply with the new banking regulations.

Legal and regulatory framework.   The Grand National Assembly presented the Accounting and Central Bank Laws for legislation in April and June 1991, although they have not yet passed. In addition, the Bulgarian government has already submitted to the Grand National Assembly the Bank and Credit Activity Law (Banking Law). Together these laws are to provide the legal framework for the operation of the financial system. In concert, the National Bank's Banking Supervision Department is adopting supervision standards in line with market-economy standards and recruiting personnel capable of undertaking on- and off-site bank inspections.

Restructuring of banks' bad loans.   To deal with the banks' nonperforming loans, the government has agreed to provide guarantees on all unproductive loans granted to enterprises before December 31, 1990 (estimated at 17 billion leva), plus any interest capitalized on such loans since January 1, 1991. To compensate for the cash-flow effect of the guarantees, the banks will be allowed to capitalize the interest on National Bank deposits. Banks will remain responsible for collecting the guaranteed loans and will be prohibited from lending to enterprises that are in arrears with banks. Later, based on portfolio reviews, the government may decide which guaranteed loans are to be written off and which should be covered by government bonds.

The Bulgarian government envisages bank privatization as a gradual process. The BCC will be able to sell bank shares to foreign parties or enter into joint ventures with foreign parties only after the merger program has been completed and after a proper valuation of banks' shares. Domestic investors will have to wait for banks to be financially restructured and audited by independent auditors, and for the National Bank Supervision Department to be fully satisfied that the bank in question is financially viable. These institutional measures are in the process of implementation, and although it will take some time before they become operational, they constitute a step forward in reforming the financial system. The most crucial elements of these measures are: (1) the pace of the reform and the role assigned to the financial system in the economic transformation process, and (2) the proposed scheme for restructuring banks' bad loans. But Bulgaria is not the only country that has adopted such measures; they are common features of financial reforms elsewhere in Eastern Europe. For that reason, the following section analyzes alternative strategies for reforming financial systems in Eastern Europe.

Alternative Strategies for Financial Reform

The governments of the East European countries have a choice between two different strategies for reforming their financial systems. These strategies differ in the pace of bank restructuring and privatization and in the methods of resolving the issue of nonperforming loans. The objective in reforming the financial system should be to transform it into an active instrument for prompting a strong supply response. This section focuses on the objectives of reforming the financial system and the positive and negative aspects of the two different strategies for privatizing banks and dealing with troubled bank loans.

To be effective, a financial reform strategy should combine quick privatization of banks and a separate scheme for guaranteeing nonperforming loans. Optimally, this strategy should ensure efficient allocation of resources. Private, restructured banks would be more efficient in allocating financial resources to the sectors that would sustain the supply response. The reform strategy should also enforce greater financial discipline on banks and enterprises. Banks should screen proposed projects more efficiently and contribute to the efficiency of enterprise management. The essence of this strategy is to minimize the use of fiscal resources. A strategy that relies on substantial fiscal resources could be impractical because such resources are scarce early in the process of economic transformation.

OBJECTIVES IN REFORMING THE FINANCIAL SYSTEM

The objective in reforming an East European country's financial system should be to change it from the passive role common in centrally planned economies to the active role characteristic of market economies. Financial sector reform, in combination with enterprise reform, should lead to a strong supply response by: (1) developing an active banking system that allocates credit efficiently and exerts financial control on enterprises, and (2) designing a scheme for dealing efficiently with banks' bad loans and minimizing their macro- and microeconomic costs. By contrast, most East European countries have adopted a gradual approach in the reform of their financial systems, maintaining the system's previous passive role.

A strong supply response in Eastern Europe requires an active banking system that efficiently allocates credit and exerts financial control over enterprises. Credit is a key element as enterprises develop and respond to market incentives. Like enterprises, banks should respond to changes in relative prices by allocating credit to enterprises that will sustain economic growth, while at the same time reducing their exposure from loss-generating enterprises and enterprises that are not viable at the new, relative prices. By doing this, banks would make credit available to the viable enterprises and impose a hard-budget constraint. By allocating credit efficiently, banks could distinguish "good" from "bad" enterprises and force the "bad" enterprises into re-structuring or liquidation. This would constitute a radical change in the role assigned to the banking system in centrally planned economies, where individual banks had no discretion in credit allocation.

In East European economies, an important action in making the financial system contribute to the supply response would be to deal efficiently with banks' bad loans, and thus reduce their macro- and microeconomic costs. A large portion of bad loans in banks' portfolios could lead to credit misallocation, and result in higher fiscal costs and bank failures. While the fiscal costs have important macroeconomic consequences, bank failures have important microeconomic consequences.

The existence of a large proportion of bad loans in East European financial systems could distort the overall economic transformation by misallocating credit. Briefly, banks with a large share of bad loans would tend to minimize the income shortfall that arises from holding bad loans by lending to "bad" enterprises as a way of turning their old, bad loans into "good" ones and avoid the need to make provisions for their bad loans, as in the well-known practice of "evergreening loans." Or they might increase their cash flow by engaging in more risky lending and enlarge the spread between their average lending and deposit rates. As other countries' experiences show,[15] this practice prevents the supply response because banks allocate credit to "bad" enterprises rather than to enterprises that would sustain growth. This crowds out production and investment by "good" enterprises by increasing the cost of credit. Such behavior could result in more, rather than fewer, bad loans. Because in Eastern Europe both banks and enterprises are publicly owned, an increase in bad loans would directly result in a higher fiscal cost, which could have important macroeconomic consequences. In addition, the increase in troubled loans would eventually make the banks less liquid and lead the banks into bankruptcy. The banks' failure, in combination with the misallocation of credit, would have important microeconomic consequences. The most evident consequences would be the credit misallocation referred to above, but the resultant loss of confidence among savers and investors would also have serious repercussions.

The problems associated with bad loans illustrate the importance of designing an efficient strategy for reforming the financial system. In particular, the pace of bank restructuring and the method for dealing with banks' bad loans would determine the role of the financial system in the supply response and in the overall transformation. In the following two sections, alternative strategies for reforming the financial system and for dealing with troubled bank loans are discussed, as well as the importance of establishing a legal framework that regulates banking activity and an institutional reform for regaining control of banks (i.e., establishment of the Bank Consolidation Company).

THE PACE OF BANK RESTRUCTURING AND PRIVATIZATION

There are two alternative strategies for setting the pace of bank restructuring and privatization. The first is to start the process of bank restructuring and privatization only after enterprise privatization has taken place. The second is to opt for a quick privatization of banks and to link it to the privatization of enterprises. With the first option, the emphasis is on enterprise restructuring and privatization, in which banks would play a passive role. This assumes that the banking system cannot become efficient unless the enterprise problems are solved. With the second option, the emphasis is on the banks' role in contributing to the supply response and to overcoming the problems of enterprises. This could be accomplished by quickly privatizing banks and restructuring the financial system. With the first option, some ad hoc privatization agency would be solely responsible for imposing strict controls on enterprises; with the second, the privatized banks in coordination with the privatization agency would have this role. Banks would control credit by allocating credit exclusively to creditworthy enterprises and by participating, in coordination with the privatization agency, in the restructuring and privatization of state-owned enterprises.

Restructuring and then privatizing banks.   The strategy of restructuring followed by privatization is based on the contention that the true value of nonperforming loans can only be ascertained when banks and enterprises are audited per Western standards, and when the privatization and restructuring of enterprises has already taken place. Uncertainty concerning the true value of unproductive bank assets could prevent private investors from investing in banks but, more important, it would become more costly for the authorities to sell banks in these conditions if the portfolio were in worse shape than anticipated. Other countries' experiences (mainly the United States') suggest that when banks with large nonperforming loans are sold to private investors, portfolio problems worsen, and the cost of cleaning up the nonperforming portfolio increases. This is because banks with large unproductive loans tend to degrade the quality of their loans even further by lending to their bad customers and engaging in still more risky activities. Because of these difficulties, this strategy calls for bank restructuring and privatization only after the true extent of the nonperforming portfolio is known. This reappraisal and restructuring could require as much as five years. An important component of the restructuring would be the cleanup of bad portfolios and some type of recapitalization. The authorities would also need to merge some banks in order to reduce the number of very small banks which might not stay profitable. Regulation would allow banks to operate as universal banks. Ownership of banks would be transferred to a holding company with total public-sector ownership, but the banks would be run as if they were private enterprises. During restructuring, the authorities would work on overcoming most of the problems that made these banks inefficient. The most important steps in restructuring would be to bring in new management, retrain incumbent managers, and reorganize banks so that they could manage risk and liability efficiently. Bank restructuring would be further stimulated through new regulations and more stringent supervision.

Quick privatization of banks.   While recognizing the effects of nonperforming assets on banks' net worth, the strategy of quick privatization acknowledges that the financial system is essential to stimulating a positive supply response. Such a response can be achieved by dividing the banking system into two groups of banks. The first group would be privatized quickly and encouraged to lend exclusively to the emerging private sector. A second group would be privatized more slowly and converted into investment banks. The first group would have the task of allocating credit to the private sector, which would be responsible for sustaining the supply response. The second group of banks (the investment banks) would have the task of contributing to the restructuring of enterprises. The role of the investment banks would be to make the sale of enterprises or their assets attractive to potential private investors (e.g., market-makers), while the government agency in charge of enterprise privatization would be responsible for making the government's policies operative. The role proposed for the investment banks represents an attempt to emulate the role of the U.S. investment banks before the Glass-Steagall Act of 1934 and of the London merchant banks. It is also an attempt to emulate the success of German and Japanese banks in the restructuring and privatization of enterprises.[16]

In the case of Bulgaria, the banks chosen for privatization could be the fifty-nine common commercial banks, while those chosen for conversion into investment banks could be the specialized commercial banks.[17] There are two main reasons for this. First, by selecting the common commercial banks for rapid privatization, the authorities could quickly reorganize the financial system. This reorganization could be accomplished by merging these banks before their privatization into five or six medium-sized banks. This would allow the authorities to reduce the large number of banks while increasing each bank's size. To make banks more attractive to private buyers, the authorities should allow investors to decide how to merge the banks. Specialized commercial banks could be converted into investment banks because these banks can take advantage of enterprises' great dependence on them to impose financial discipline and force their restructuring. Second, the common commercial banks have fewer loans—evidence suggests that they have fewer bad loans as well—while specialized commercial banks hold not only more total loans but more bad loans. This situation would minimize the immediate fiscal cost of the bank privatization strategy.

The quick-privatization strategy, unlike the restructure-and-then-privatize strategy, does not require the valuation of banks' bad loans as a precondition for privatization. It argues that the authorities should be willing to remove all loans that the private investor would classify as troubled, and that this should be done at the moment of privatization. By leaving only the good loans, the authorities would assure more efficient management of the privatized banks. This has been an important lesson from other countries' experiences with bank privatization.[18] In addition, separating out the bad loans would enable the authorities to accelerate the privatization of banks because the pricing of nonperforming loans is one of the most serious impediments to completion of this process.

The authorities can assure quick privatization of banks and guarantee the establishment of sound banks by creating an excess demand from private buyers. Banks should be offered to both foreign and domestic investors or to any combination of the two. Excess demand for private banks should enable the authorities to screen private buyers, and could be generated by limiting the number of banks and by offering incentives. Such incentives should include the cleanup of bad loans (as explained before) and the removal of any excess personnel (a process to be negotiated with private buyers). As minimum conditions, monetary authorities should require that private buyers: (1) comply with the minimum capital criteria by bringing in fresh money, (2) bring a team of experienced bankers, (3) observe all regulations, (4) lend exclusively to the private sector, (5) limit any lending to bank shareholders, and (6) comply with loan concentration limits to be established by the new banking law. Similar criteria can be established for the later privatization of the specialized commercial banks.

The strategy of quick privatization of banks has several advantages over the strategy of restructuring first and privatizing later. The four most significant advantages are more efficient allocation of credit, greater incentive to save, more efficient restructuring of enterprises, and better risk management.

More efficient allocation of credit would be accomplished by encouraging privatized banks to lend exclusively to the private sector, a practice that would strengthen the supply response. The combination of restructured banks under the control of the public sector (direct or indirect) with very tight credit policy results in very little credit allocated to the private sector. This crowds out private-sector supply response, as has been shown in countries further along in the reform process, such as Poland. Three factors contribute to this result. First, available financial resources shrink as a consequence of high inflation. Therefore, fewer resources are available for lending. Second, most of the resources of the banks being restructured are frozen in the loss-generating enterprises, and it becomes difficult for these banks to be repaid. Moreover, new regulations imposing higher capital requirements and provisioning on loans in difficulties (not yet classified as nonperforming) make it more difficult for these banks to recover their loans. (This is even assuming that most nonperforming loans would be removed.) If banks force enterprises to repay their loans, enterprises might decide to default and banks would be unable to meet capital and provisioning requirements. But if banks continue lending to these enterprises, evergreening their loans in the belief that one day the enterprises would be able to repay their loans, then they can increase their profits and meet the capital and provisioning requirements. Third, the public sector absorbs most of the available financial resources either to finance its own deficit, which is difficult to control, or to finance existing preferential credit schemes.

Private savers probably will distrust the banking system because they lost most of their savings when prices were adjusted. Because a strong supply response depends on increased savings, *greater incentives to save must be created.* This can best be done by creating private banks and radically changing the old financial system. By bringing new management and technologies, private banks can offer a greater range of banking services in a more competitive environment.

More efficient restructuring of enterprises would be accomplished by dividing the banking system and forcing bank specialization. First, private banks would be specialized in supporting the emerging private sector and providing resources to investors willing to buy all or part of any of the enterprises. Second, private investment banks could take advantage of enterprises' loans to impose financial discipline and to influence the enterprises' managerial decisions. Financial discipline can be imposed by forcing enterprises that fail to service their debt into liquidation or restructuring. Moreover, these private banks could participate in enterprise privatization by selling bad loans to private Western investors at a discount. This, however, would require close coordination with the government agency in charge of privatization. One advantage of this system would be that it would accelerate the process of enterprise privatization by avoiding the liquidation of property through foreclosure as has been done in Germany and Japan in the process of enterprise restructuring and privatization.[19]

Banks run by private owners would be *more effective at managing risk* and more capable of bringing in new management because private capital would be at risk. It is arguable whether the appointed managers and board of directors of banks brought in as part of the strategy to restructure banks first and privatize later would behave similarly.

There are risks in pursuing quick bank privatization. First is the risk of banks accumulating bad loans as a result of economic instability during the transition to a market economy. During this period, there will be great uncertainty about the prospects of enterprises, some of which will fail. Second is the risk of failing to find private buyers for these banks. This could happen because the private sector is very small, because there are few experienced bankers, or because potential buyers may lack the resources to buy a bank. Moreover, it could be argued that the individuals who own the resources might not be suitable bankers because they accumulated their wealth illegally. The quick-privatization strategy provides some flexibility by allowing both domestic and foreign investors to be buyers. If the availability of resources is the constraint, monetary authorities can propose joint ventures with other domestic and foreign buyers, or can develop a scheme that would enable potential buyers to procure the resources. The third risk is that private banks will not find enough creditworthy private enterprises. Perhaps this is the more serious problem because banks involved in restructuring will find it difficult to assess risk, and because new private enterprises will have few assets that can be used as collateral. The authorities, however, could use at least two schemes to minimize this problem. The first involves establishing a register of creditworthy private entrepreneurs accessible to banks via direct computer lines. The second involves allowing banks to use or accept other assets as collateral.

Strategies for Dealing with Nonperforming Loans

In dealing with nonperforming loans, there are also two options. The authorities could either remove nonperforming loans from banks' balance sheets and transfer them to a new institution responsible for their collection, or provide guarantees on banks' nonperforming loans and leave them off the balance sheet.

Removing nonperforming loans.   There are two reasons for completely removing unproductive loans from banks. The first is to avoid possible moral dilemma. A mix of good and bad clients served by the same bank could cause good clients to turn into bad ones. It would be difficult for bankers to impose financial discipline on their sound clients while allowing more leeway to their less stable clients. Second, removing bad loans makes efficient practices more evident. Bank efficiency would depend on the ability of managers to minimize risk. These managers would be judged on their lending practices and not on their ability to collect loans that were awarded under very different management and for political purposes. The major disadvantage to this strategy is that it could be very expensive to collect these nonperforming loans once they are removed from the banks.

Guaranteeing nonperforming loans. There are two reasons to guarantee troubled loans. The first is to impose financial discipline on all borrowers and use this pressure to force the restructuring of enterprises. This can only be done by linking the investment bank with the enterprise-restructuring processes, otherwise enterprises are not motivated to restructure. The second reason is to minimize the fiscal costs of dealing with the nonperforming loans. This can be done by offering price incentives to banks that collect these unproductive loans. For example, banks could earn a commission on the amount collected. This price incentive should only be offered to the investment banks that become private as an additional incentive to take a portion of the nonperforming assets. The major disadvantages of offering incentives are the accompanying moral hazards and the lack of transparency in bank management.[20] While these schemes differ in terms of where the loans are placed, they are similar in how they convert bad bank loans into public-sector debt. First, monetary authorities need to clear off the National Bank's deposits that guarantee specialized commercial banks' nonperforming loans and clean up the Foreign Trade Bank's foreign-exchange losses by substituting the National Bank's deposits held by specialized commercial banks and the Foreign Trade Bank's foreign-exchange losses for two types of government bonds. The authorities should issue one type of bond to remove the National Bank's deposits held by specialized commercial banks and thus free monetary policy from being affected by the size of enterprises' nonperforming loans. By doing this, the authorities could convert the National Bank's deposits held by specialized commercial banks into public-sector domestic debt. A second type of bond would be a device for transferring the public-sector foreign debt held by the Foreign Trade Bank to the Treasury. The authorities should substitute the Foreign Trade Bank's foreign-exchange liabilities and foreign-exchange losses for government bonds. This measure would effectively transfer the cost of the foreign-exchange losses to the budget and would enable the Foreign Trade Bank to operate like any other commercial bank.

The key difference between the two schemes is the treatment of nonproductive loans. By pursuing the option of removing all bad loans, commercial banks would transfer such loans to a newly established institution that specializes in collecting bad loans. Per this option, banks would transfer both the nonperforming bad loans and the National Bank deposits. By taking the option of guaranteeing nonperforming loans, banks would simply shift both the nonperforming loans and National Bank deposits to an off–balance-sheet item. Any amount that banks collected on these nonperforming loans would then be transferred directly to the budget because the Treasury would have already covered the National Bank for the amount of its deposits.

Providing loan guarantees has several advantages over the complete removal of unproductive loans. With the guarantee option, experienced private bankers would be responsible for collecting bad loans. Price incentives would play a key role in the guarantee option in encouraging the collection of such loans. With the removal of bad loans, however, a new institution would be created with little knowledge of the history of these unproductive loans, and this new institution would lack overall banking experience. Its employees would be quasi-governmental, and would lack the incentives provided by the private sector. Moreover, the option in which nonperforming loans are removed lacks price incentives.

Conclusion

Bulgarian authorities have attempted to correct the short-term problems of their financial system, but most of the identified structural obstacles remain. Correction of these problems requires comprehensive reform of the financial system. The best way to accomplish this is to undertake quick privatization of banks and link this process to the promotion of private enterprises. This strategy would foster the necessary supply-side response.

Notes

[1]Despite recent government measures, most of these structural problems remain. Currently, the authorities are discussing strategies for reforming the financial system.

[2]One CCB, the Sofia Bank, accounts for 26 percent of total CCB deposits and 43 percent of total assets.

[3]Roberto de Rezende Rocha, "Inflation and Stabilization in Yugoslavia," PRE Working Paper Series, no. 752 (Washington, D.C.: The World Bank).

[4]Estimates indicate that a "quick" transaction can take fifteen days; others take about a year.

[5]This estimate is close to the government's estimate, calculated by the NBB's Supervision Department using commercial banks' balance sheets. This estimate, like the author's, is subject to the problems mentioned in the text because it was done before the introduction of new banking regulation and supervision.

[6]In addition, it could be argued that commercial banks would refrain from paying back these deposits because they are guaranteeing the nonperforming loans granted by the NBB. Moreover, the implicit NBB guarantee on these deposits presents a moral hazard. Because banks are the property of state-owned enterprises, enterprise managers would try to maximize their benefit from the guarantee by forcing a write-off of an enterprise loan in the same amount as NBB deposits.

[7]This is because the NBB has no other sources from which to finance its cash-flow deficit. The NBB cannot increase further reserve requirements on the SSB (it is committed to reduce them), and the availability of foreign finance is limited.

[8]Net foreign-exchange liabilities are the difference between foreign-exchange liabilities and foreign-exchange assets, including government foreign-exchange credits as part of the foreign-exchange assets.

[9]There are, however, some indications that the fall in the M2-to-GDP ratio had the effect of overstating the true extent of the monetary overhang. This is partly explained by the fact that the increase in the price level was greater than anticipated. Although this situation would require further research, one can argue that monetary policy was extremely restrictive. Nominal credit ceilings (calculated on the basis of an estimated *equilibrium* nominal demand for money) resulted in a nominal expansion in the supply of money below what would be required for the full adjustment in relative prices to take place. In fact, one can assume that in the context of Eastern Europe, the initial increase in the price level is exogenous (determined by the adjustment in relative prices), and if monetary policy is too restrictive, the money market would clear by adjusting income downwards. This is the way to reduce the demand for money to the supply level, as the sharp recession of 1991 showed.

[10]To minimize the effect of the increase in interest rates on banks' balance sheets, the authorities drafted an old loans law that provides for the change in interest rates on loan contracts made before February 1991. The only exceptions to this law to date are the old mortgages and consumer loans.

[11]The program provides for a reduction in the government budget from an estimated 13 percent of GDP in 1990 to 3.5 percent in 1991.

[12]The NBB only operates as a monitoring and information agency to which banks must report their foreign-exchange positions and exchange rates offered.

[13]The NBB is negotiating the repayment of part of SSB's credits. But this is difficult because, as discussed earlier, the NBB used these credits to finance commercial banks' nonperforming loans.

[14]The government also accumulated credit as a way of financing its deficit.

[15]For a review of other countries' experiences, see M. Hinds, *Economic Effects of Financial Crises*, PRE Working Paper Series, no. 104 (Washington, D.C.: The World Bank, October 1988); A. de Juan, *From Good Bankers to Bad Bankers: Ineffective Supervision and Management Deterioration as Major Elements in Banking Crises* (Washington, D.C.: The World Bank, June 1987); and A. Thorne, *Why a Market Solution to Financial Crises Might Be Feasible: The Case of Restructuring of Financial Systems through the Analysis of Twelve Cases* (Washington, D.C.: The World Bank, October 1988).

[16]For a similar proposal, see L. J. Brainard, *The Financial Sector in the Transition to a Market Economy: How to Reform Eastern Europe's Banking Systems* (Washington, D.C.: The World Bank, n.d.). For an illuminating discussion of the role of U.S. investment banks before the Glass-Steagall Act and of the London merchant banks, see R. Chernow, *The House of Morgan: An American Banking Dynasty and the Rise of Modern Finance* (New York: Simon and Schuster, 1991). For the role of banks in Germany and Japan and their role in enterprise restructuring and privatization, see C. Mayer, "The Assessment: Financial Systems and Corporate Investment," *Oxford Review of Economic Policy*, 3(4): i–xvi, and "Financial Systems, Corporate Finance, and Economic Development," in G. Hubbard, ed., *Information, Capital Markets, and Investment* (Chicago, Ill.: National Bureau of Economic Research, 1990); J. Corbett, "International Perspectives on Financing: Evidence from Japan," *Oxford Review of Economic Policy*, 3(4): 30–55; and J. S. S. Edwards and K. Fischer, *Banks, Finance, and Investment in West Germany since 1970*, Discussion Paper No. 4 (London: Centre for Economic Policy Research, January 1991).

[17]Although its applicability to Bulgaria is illustrated here, this strategy can easily be applied to many other East European countries. For instance, in Poland one could select the state-owned commercial banks for quick privatization and the specialized banks for conversion into investment banks.

[18]The Spanish experience with bank restructuring provides a positive example, while a negative example is provided by the case of the United States savings and loans.

[19]This was also the experience of some U.S. banks before the 1930s, such as the J.P. Morgan Bank. For an illuminating account of the role of the Morgan bank in the consolidation and restructuring process of U.S. firms, see Chernow, *The House of Morgan*.

[20]This price-incentive scheme differs in several ways from the one proposed by the Bulgarian authorities: (1) it only provides guarantees and does not combine them with government bonds; (2) it does not allow interest capitalization on bad loans or on NBB deposits on banks; (3) it enables banks in direct negotiation with their client enterprises to determine the portion of loans to be written off, whereas in the case of Bulgaria the enterprise restructuring agency determines how much of the loan will be written off; and (4) it combines incentives for collecting nonperforming loans with the private property of banks.

Appendix: A Note on Financial Data Problems

This chapter's analysis is based on banks' reported balance sheets and financial statements. As is recognized in Bulgaria, these data are subject to several flaws, which arise from:

1. *Differences in accounting plans.* Bank accounting plans in Bulgaria are different from those in Western countries. This raises issues of classification and interpretation. Presently, in Bulgaria, there are three different accounting plans: one for the National Bank of Bulgaria (NBB), another for the Bulgarian Foreign Trade Bank (FTB), and another for the commercial banks. These differences contribute to poor data quality.

2. *Assets and liabilities valuations.* Assets and liabilities valuation is another source of problems, as it introduces distortions in bank balance sheets. It is a particular problem with fixed assets, loans, and foreign currency operations. Fixed assets, for example, real estate, have experienced a surge in prices which is unaccounted for in bank balance sheets; banks are carrying a large proportion of unproductive loans which are not provisioned for; and foreign currency operations are valued at the official exchange rate while such transactions take place at the more depreciated commercial exchange rate. In addition, banks hold substantial volumes of unsettled assets and liabilities due to delays in the clearing system. These unsettled assets and liabilities have had the consequence of overstating the true size of bank balance sheets.

3. *Macroeconomic distortions.* Macroeconomic distortions consist of price, interest rate, and exchange rate controls. These controls affect bank balance sheets and financial statements by distorting the true value of assets and liabilities.

In cases where data are weak, the author has avoided comparisons with other countries or refrained from using the data, and in cases where sources of problems were known, corrections have been made. Conclusions based on these data should be regarded as preliminary.

Editor and Contributors

Dirk W. Damrau is Vice President of the Global Emerging Markets Research Group at Salomon Brothers, Inc. He was awarded an M.A. by the Woodrow Wilson International School of Public Affairs, Princeton, New Jersey, in 1987. He has written numerous articles on the emerging markets and investment opportunities in Eastern Europe and the republics of the former Soviet Union, published by Salomon Brothers.

Marvin R. Jackson is Professor and Director of the Leuven Institute for Central and East European Studies at the Catholic University in Leuven, Belgium. Prior to holding this post, he was Deputy Director of Research for Radio Free Europe/Radio Liberty in Munich, Germany, and Professor of Economics at Arizona State University. He has written extensively on economics, and is the author of *Economic Systems: Institutional Differences and Changes* (forthcoming 1992), editor of *East-South Trade: Economics and Political Economics* (1985), and coauthor with John R. Lampe of *Balkan Economic Development, 1550–1950: From Imperial Borderlands to Southeastern European States* (1982). Among his numerous journal articles is "Constraints on Systemic Transformation and Their Policy Implications," *Oxford Review of Economic Policy*, Winter 1991. He received a Ph.D. in economics from the University of California, Berkeley, in 1962.

John R. Lampe, Director of East European Studies at the Woodrow Wilson International Center for Scholars in Washington, D.C., since 1987, is also Professor of History at the University of Maryland, College Park. He received his B.A. from Harvard University and his M.A. from the University of Minnesota, both in economics, and his Ph.D. in 1971 from the University of Wisconsin in European economic history. He served as a Foreign Service Officer in Yugoslavia and Bulgaria from 1964 to 1967. He is coauthor with Marvin R. Jackson of *Balkan Economic History, 1550–1950: From Imperial Borderlands to Developing Nations* (1982), which won the Vucinich Prize of the American Association for the Advancement of Slavic Studies, author of *The Bulgarian Economy in the 20th Century* (1986); coauthor of *Yugoslav-American Economic Relations since World War II* (1990); and has written numerous articles on East European economic history and current development, which are his primary areas of interest for research.

Maurice E. May, a portfolio manager and securities analyst with Gardner & Preston Moss, Inc., has worked in finance since 1976. He received a B.A. in history from the University of Maryland, College Park, and is a member of the Boston Security Analyst's Society.

József Rotyis is the Deputy Chief Executive Officer for the Budapest Stock Exchange and project manager for the Hungarian Clearing and Depository Center project of the BSE. From 1989 to 1990, he was Deputy General Manager of the capital market department of the National Bank of Hungary. He has published various articles in the Hungarian professional press on monetary policy, capital markets, and money exchange. After graduating from the University of Economics in Budapest in 1983, Rotyis pursued postgraduate studies at the International Monetary Fund in Washington, D.C., London University, and the City of London Polytechnic University.

Alice Teichova is Emeritus Professor of Economic History, Honorary Fellow of Girton College, Cambridge (England), and Senior Research Associate of the London School of Economics and Political Science.

Alfredo Thorne has been with the World Bank, EMENA Technical Department, Trade and Finance Division (EMTTF) since 1987, and is working on domestic finances and microeconomic issues for Europe, Central Asia, the Middle East, and North Africa (ECA/EMENA). He was awarded a Ph.D. (economics) in 1986 by Oxford University, England. Among his numerous publications is *Issues in Reforming Financial Systems in Eastern Europe: The Case of Bulgaria*, PRE Working Paper Series No. 882 (World Bank, April 1992).

Index

Page numbers in italics refer to tables.

109